A NOTE *from*

At the conclusion of this book, I had just returned from the Middle East and a meeting with Prime Minister Benjamin Netanyahu and President Reuven Rivlin of Israel. As part of a special delegation, I also met with President Abdel Fattah el-Sisi of Egypt and King Abdullah of Jordan.

Following that we later convened in Jordan, where it was our privilege to meet with leaders of the Evangelical churches there. Virtually every leader had been interrogated by the Jordanian General Intelligence Department and was asked the same question: "Are you preaching Jesus to Muslims?"

The pastor of the only English-speaking congregation in Amman was given eight weeks to leave the country. He was praying earnestly for a miracle. When we met with King Abdullah over lunch, I made an appeal to the king on behalf of the pastors and Evangelical leaders. The king very enthusiastically responded.

I said to King Abdullah, "You have just answered a great prayer that the church has been praying. God bless you."

Before flying to Jordan, we had flown to Egypt for a session with President el-Sisi. En route, I prayed for a word from God for the president. When we met, I was prompted to say to him, "Your Excellency, you saved Egypt from the Muslim Brotherhood. Fighting terror is a human right." Everyone in the room broke out in applause.

The following day, he delivered a speech at a world summit. President el-Sisi boldly declared, "Fighting terror is a human right." Since that time, my words to him have appeared in over one hundred newspapers in the Muslim world. God indeed answers prayer!

I pray that as a result of your having read this book, you will not only pray but also receive a multitude of answers to your prayers as your faith grows.

Mike Evans

PRAYER
A CONVERSATION *with* GOD

#1 *NEW YORK TIMES* BESTSELLING AUTHOR
MIKE EVANS

P.O. BOX 30000, PHOENIX, AZ 85046

Prayer: A Conversation with God
Copyright 2018 by Time Worthy Books
P. O. Box 30000, Phoenix, AZ 85046

Unless otherwise indicated, scripture references are taken
from the ***New King James Version***, Copyright © 1982 by Thomas Nelson, Inc.
Used by permission. All rights reserved.

Unless otherwise indicated, scripture references are taken from ***The Holy Bible,
New International Version***®, NIV® Copyright ©1973, 1978, 1984, 2011 by Biblica, Inc.®
Used by permission. All rights reserved worldwide."

Scripture quotations marked ASV are taken from ***The Holy Bible,
American Standard Version.*** Copyright © 1901 by Public Domain.

Scripture quotations marked ESV are taken from ***The Holy Bible, English Standard Version***,
copyright © 2001 by Crossway Bibles, a division of Good News Publishers.
Used by permission. All rights reserved.

Scripture quotations marked KJV are taken from
King James Version, Public Domain.

Scripture quotations marked NASB are taken from the ***New American Standard Bible***.
Copyright © 1960, 1962, 1963, 1968, 1971, 1972, 1973, 1975, 1977, 1995 by The Lockman Foundation.
Used by permission. www.Lockman.org

Scripture quotations marked NLT are taken from the ***Holy Bible, New Living Translation***.
Copyright © 1996, 2004, 2007. Used by permission of Tyndale House Publishers Inc.,
Carol Stream, Illinois 60188. All rights reserved.

Scripture quotations marked RSV are taken from the ***Revised Standard Version of the Bible***.
Copyright © 1946, 1952, and 1971 the Division of Christian Education of the National Council of the
Churches of Christ in the United States of America. Used by permission. All rights reserved.

Scripture quotations marked NET are taken from ***The NET Bible®, New English Translation***
Copyright © 1996 By Biblical Studies Press, L.L.C.
NET Bible® is a registered trademark The NET Bible® Logo, Service Mark
Copyright © 1997 by Biblical Studies Press, L.L.C. All rights reserved.

Scripture quotations marked CSB (Christian Standard Bible) are taken from
Blue Letter Bible. "Book of 1 Samuel 1". Blue Letter Bible. 1996–2017. 28 Sep 2017

Scripture quotations marked HNV are taken from
The Hebrew Names Version, Public Domain.

Scripture quotations marked TLB are taken from ***The Living Bible***
Copyright © 1971 by Tyndale House Foundation. Used by permission of
Tyndale House Publishers Inc., Carol Stream, Illinois 60188. All rights reserved.

Hardcover:	978-1-62961-162-4
Paperback:	978-1-62961-161-7
Canada:	978-1-62961-163-1

All rights reserved. No portion of this book may be reproduced, stored in a retrieval system,
or transmitted in any form or by any means—electronic, mechanical, photocopy, recording, or any other—
except for brief quotations in printed reviews, without the prior permission of the publisher.

This book is dedicated to
Casper ten Boom
and his courageous family,
including his daughters, Betsie
who died in Ravensbruck concentration camp,
and Corrie, who carried the message of faith
and forgiveness worldwide.

In 1844, Casper's great-great-grandfather,
a Christian Zionist, began a weekly meeting
to pray for the peace of Jerusalem (Psalm 122:6).
Casper took up the banner and continued the meetings;
the ten Boom family and others who stopped by
prayed specifically for the Jewish people
and the rebirth of the nation of Israel.

The meetings ended on February 28, 1944,
one hundred years later, when Nazi soldiers raided the
ten Boom home to arrest the family for aiding Dutch Jews.
The Jerusalem Prayer Team resumed the prayer meeting,
and now has 34 million members, the world's largest
prayer group and the top Facebook site in Christianity.

In 1988, I arranged for the purchase of the
ten Boom home in Haarlem, Holland, restored it,
and am now chairman of the board of the
Corrie ten Boom museum, a part of our global ministry.

*For we were so utterly burdened beyond
our strength that we despaired of life itself.*

—2 Corinthians 1:8b esv

At the age of eleven, I had no thought of being commissioned by God to do anything. My first and last thoughts each day were of survival. Would I be able to withstand my father's brutality, to stay alive one more day?

After sustaining yet another severe beating and choking at the age of eleven, despair overwhelmed me as I lay on the floor of my bedroom wallowing in my own vomit and writhing in pain. It was then that I prayed my first conscious prayer—not of thanksgiving, not of petition, not of intercession, but of despair! My goal in life up to that moment had been to reach the age of twenty; I was certain my father would kill me before then. At that moment, I realized my prayer to reach that ripe old age was in danger of being cut short. Instead of that becoming the darkest day of my life, however, it became the brightest.

With tears streaming down my face, I looked heavenward and cried, "God, why was I born? Why?"

Moments before praying that prayer, my father had returned home from a night of drinking in a drunken stupor.

Surely I had not been born just to be a punching bag for a bigoted, alcoholic father. As quickly as I had whispered those words, the room was flooded with a light so brilliant it blinded me. It reminded me of a giant spotlight—the kind you see tracing its light across the night skies. My terror was uncontrollable. I thought Dad had come back to finish the job. He was going to beat me to death, and this time I would not escape. I heard a noise that sounded like a wounded puppy's whine and realized the whimper was coming from my own throat. My first thought was to crawl under the bed to protect myself, certain I was about to be the victim of his steel-toed boots.

I covered my face with my hands and closed my eyes as tightly as I could squeeze them. After what seemed like an eon, I realized there was no other sound in the room other than my pain-induced moan. Surely, my father would have already been screaming and cursing, fists flailing. Now there was only that brilliant light. I slowly spread my fingers and eased my swollen eyes open as imperceptibly as possible. I was hoping to see an empty room.

That dazzling light would change my life forever. Although it was not meant to be a prayer, God had heard my cry and answered the anguish of my heart with His very presence. There, lying on my bedroom floor, I was about to discover who I really was—a beloved child of God, valued, treasured, priceless. This revelation was joy unspeakable.

The light was so vivid it was like looking at the sun but didn't blind me or hurt my eyes. Instead, it produced a warm glow that filled the very core of my being. The light revealed that my father was no longer standing over me, poised to inflict more pain. I could no longer hear his threats; I could no longer see the rage on his drunken and blotchy face. Yes, Someone was there, but the presence was not threatening; it was reassuring. Without being aware of having made that assessment, I felt safe and secure.

Where there had been agonizing pain and paralyzing fear, now there was a supernatural energy. Before the light infiltrated my room, I was depressed, demoralized, and distressed. Where there had been darkness, there was now light—radiant white light. Not a single corner of the room escaped its warming rays.

Terror gripped me as I saw two arms reaching for me. With almost supernatural clarity, I realized those were not Dad's arms. As I looked more closely, I realized that in the center of each wrist was a horrific, jagged scar. It appeared as though each one had been snagged and then ripped open by something large and pointed. Slowly it dawned on me that I had seen pictures of very similar scars on the leaflets we had been given in Sunday school on Easter. Was I hallucinating; or had I gone completely crazy? Jesus would not—could not—be in my bedroom. My mind tried to grasp what was happening. I must have thought

I was having a complete nervous breakdown. That would have explained it.

Something else suddenly occurred to me: Where had my fear gone? Maybe Dad had achieved his purpose—to kill the "bastard" in his house. How could the vision I was seeing be possible otherwise? How else could I experience such power and peace unless . . . was I dead?

My disbelieving eyes followed those arms up and up until I could see the source of the light. I saw, standing there in my bedroom, what could only be the Lord Jesus Christ. He was either clothed in light or in the most magnificent white robe imaginable—whiter than fresh snow; whiter than the clouds that floated in a sun-filled sky; whiter than anything I had ever seen. Draped from His shoulder to His waist was a deep purple cloth—more purple than the heavens at sunset.

As I lifted my head to look into His face, I was instantly drawn to His eyes. They were smiling, happy eyes filled with every color of the rainbow, and they were fixed on me! It was like looking into an illuminated bowl of the world's most highly prized jewels. I felt as if I could see through them and beyond to heaven and the promise of eternal peace. They were like magnets drawing me into their depths. Keeping His arms outstretched, He looked at me with such an expression of love. Then He spoke words I had never heard before, and His words changed my life forever. Jesus said, "Son, I love you, and I have a plan for your life."

Instantly I was delivered from all my fears, healed, saved, and called. It would be several years before I understood, theologically, the full impact of what had happened in my bedroom that bleak night. As I have dared to share the story of the atrocities I once endured, the story of a frightened, rejected little boy's terrible suffering has helped to bring healing and hope to hurting people—people struggling for perfection, performance, and praise; people with plastic smiles on their faces and gaping holes in their souls; people of all ages and from every strata of society who so desperately need to hear that a Savior with smiling eyes and nail scars loves, accepts, and values them, and that He has a wonderful plan for their lives.

As my spiritual life began to grow, expand, and mature, I uncovered others in the pages of God's Word that had prayed in despair and received a miraculous answer from Jehovah, including our Lord himself.

A prayer is not recorded for Adam and Eve, but surely they bent their faces to the earth and wailed, or perhaps they were simply rendered speechless when God proclaimed:

> The ground is cursed because of you. You will eat from it by means of painful labor all the days of your life. —Genesis 3:17b CSB

Even though God had promised a way of restoration in His pronouncement (see Genesis 3:15), Adam must have been despondent when God drove the two from Eden and then "stationed the cherubim and the flaming, whirling sword east of the garden of Eden to guard the way to the tree of life" (verse 24).

Everything that has transpired in my life has been because of prayer. One word from God changed my life forever; I realized that prayer was my words to God, but He also spoke to me through His Word. No word from His mouth has ever died. My prayer today is that your faith will soar as you read this book, and you will realize that God can turn your pain into power, purpose, and passion. He stands ready to transform your test into a testimony through the power of prayer.

My commitment to Jesus Christ has taken me not only to Israel, but to places I had never dreamed I would go—Iraq, Kurdistan, Mogadishu, the Soviet Union, Belarus, the White House, the Vatican. In those locales, I met people I never expected to meet—presidents, prime ministers, kings, generals, soldiers, beggars, atheists, and extraordinarily dedicated believers. Doors have been opened of which I had never dreamed, but not by my efforts. John the beloved apostle wrote in Revelation 3:7 (NLT):

> This is the message from the one who is holy and true, the one who has the key of David. What he opens, no one can close; and what he closes, no one can open.

The key of David was entrusted to the chamberlain or vizier of the king's palace. This symbol of authority afforded entrance into every room; nothing was hidden from the holder of the key. For the child of God, prayer is that key. It permits entrance into the very throne room of heaven—into the presence of the King of Kings and Lord of Lords.

In the desert tabernacle and later in the temple in Jerusalem, the high priest was the only individual allowed to enter the Holy of Holies, but only once each year: on Yom Kippur, the Day of Atonement. The curtain divided the priests who performed the daily activities in the Holy Place from the holy of holies. It was a barrier so that man would not casually, rashly, or disrespectfully enter into the presence of *El Hakkadosh*, the Holy God, who can not tolerate sin. Habakkuk 1:13 says of Jehovah, "Your eyes are too pure to look on evil; you cannot tolerate wrongdoing."

When Jesus breathed His last breath and gave up the ghost, Matthew tells us that "the veil of the temple was rent in twain from the top to the bottom" (Matthew 27:51 KJV). The temple's high priest must have been terribly frightened! He was likely unaware that his work was finished, that the Lamb of God had been offered sacrificially one time for the sins of all. As the high priest made his way into the Holy of Holies to sprinkle the blood of the evening sacrifice on the horns of the altar, the veil that separated man from God had been ripped from top to bottom. It was a symbol that we no longer have to wait to be represented yearly by the high priest:

> Seeing then that we have a great high priest, that is passed into the heavens, Jesus the Son of God, let us hold

fast our profession. For we have not an high priest which cannot be touched with the feeling of our infirmities; but was in all points tempted like as we are, yet without sin. Let us therefore come boldly unto the throne of grace, that we may obtain mercy, and find grace to help in time of need. —Hebrews 4:14–16 KJV

Believers now have free access into the presence of God so that "by prayer and supplication with thanksgiving let [our] requests be made known unto God" (Philippians 4:6 KJV).

The work that Jesus Christ had been sent to do was finished. The beautiful David Phelps song "End of the Beginning" says it all:

And though he never ever did a single thing wrong
the angry crowd chose Him.
And then He walked down the road and died on the cross
And that was the end of the beginning . . .
Three days later he rose!

Although specially chosen to minister in the Holy of Holies, there were exact steps that had to be undertaken by the high priest before he could safely step through the veil into the overwhelming presence of God. Now you and I as believers hold the "key" that gives us the privilege that allows us immediate access to Him to make our requests known!

I have set watchmen on your walls, O Jerusalem;
They shall never hold their peace day or night.
You who make mention of the Lord, do not keep silent,
And give Him no rest till He establishes
And till He makes Jerusalem a praise in the earth.

—ISAIAH 62:6-7

Prayer is an essential part of the life of a Believer. But just what is prayer? It has been described by some as practicing the presence of God. By others, it is defined as the abandonment of self-reliance and the admission of our need for and our total confidence in Jehovah. We humble ourselves, let our petitions rise heavenward, and release our faith and hope in almighty God. Through prayer, mere man can touch the heart of God.

When you have a great need in your life, circle it with prayer. What does that mean and how is it accomplished? It is a metaphorical circle that allows you to focus on a particular need or needs according to Philippians 4:6, "Be careful for nothing; but in every thing by prayer and supplication with thanksgiving let your requests be made known unto God" (KJV).

Prayer is not an attempt to manipulate God to our way of thinking. It is not trite, repetitious, ritualistic, or showy. Author and pastor Dr. Paul Chappell defines prayer:

> Prayer is not a show nor a ritual. Prayer is you speaking directly to the Creator of the world about your deepest needs, desires, and burdens. It's expressing your thankfulness for His goodness. It's your privilege and honor as a believer.

In the Old Testament, God uses one of the most captivating images in the Bible—a watchman. What does that have to do with prayer? How can we learn about prayer by studying the watchman? The prophet Ezekiel delivers a cautionary word of warning from Jehovah in chapter 3, verse 17 (ESV):

> Son of man, I have made you a watchman for the house of Israel. Whenever you hear a word from my mouth, you shall give them warning from me.

In chapter 33, Jehovah repeats His instructions to the prophet. The metaphor is drawn from the earliest days of agricultural societies when posts were erected overlooking crops to provide a tower for a watchman. The towers were designed to offer a view of thieves—man or animal—who would ransack the ripening harvests. For many, the harvest was a matter of life and death, of having food for the coming winter or starving. The men who were appointed as watchmen were crucial to the survival of his village.

The same was true of cities. During times of impending attacks, watchmen would scour the horizon for invaders and then sound the warning to alert inhabitants to approaching danger. The city gates would be closed and barred and defenders would take their positions on the battlements.

Just as a watchman warned the people of a coming enemy and was, therefore, the first line of defense, intercessory prayer warriors are the first line of spiritual defense for our nation and our communities. What happens when the watchmen fail to do their jobs? The prophet Ezekiel gives us insight:

> But if the watchman sees the sword coming and does not blow the trumpet to warn the people and the sword comes and takes someone's life, that person's life will be taken because of their sin, but I will hold the watchman accountable for their blood. —Ezekiel 33:6 NIV

A watchman cannot be apathetic; indifference will suffocate our faith. It must be replaced by steadfast prayer in order to revive our spiritual lives. Nothing is more important to God than prayer! God will do nothing without prayer. It is the fuel that moves the engine of humanity.

God has a purpose and a plan for our lives. The very existence of our nation and the nation of Israel are forever dependent on prayer. His will and His blessings are bound up in prayer. His purposes and plans are more important than anything man can do. Through Jeremiah the prophet, God offered: "Call to me and I will answer you and tell you great and unsearchable things you do not know" (Jeremiah 33:3 NIV).

As he prophesied to the Jewish people during their captivity in Babylon, he was given this promise:

> Thus says the LORD, the Holy One of Israel, and his Maker:
> "Ask Me of things to come concerning My sons; and concerning the work of My hands, you command Me."
> —Isaiah 45:11

The Jews were ultimately delivered from their captivity, and revival came to Israel. God takes prayer so seriously that He says we can call on Him and He *will* answer! That is His promise to us.

When the children of Israel were driven into captivity in Babylon by Nebuchadnezzar, God had a plan in place for their deliverance before the idea of invasion even entered the mind of their enemy. Freedom from their oppressors did not come quickly; the reality was that over seventy years later the children of Israel were still in captivity. What had happened? Had God forgotten to set His alarm clock? Had He slept through freeing His people? Was God on vacation? Absolutely not! Psalm 121:3b-4 reminds us of Jehovah's watchfulness:

> He who keeps you will not slumber. Behold, He who keeps Israel shall neither slumber nor sleep.

Although God had a plan for their rescue and had even given them the timetable through the prophet Jeremiah, nothing would happen until someone prayed. God's people needed an advocate on Earth to ask for the fulfillment of God's Word. James 4:2 says, "Yet you do not have because you do not ask." God's ear has always been attuned to the sound of the cries of His people, of intercessory prayer from His children. Psalm 34:15-17 assures us:

> The eyes of the LORD are on the righteous, and His ears are open to their cry. The face of the LORD is against those who do evil, to cut off the remembrance of them from the earth. The righteous cry out, and the LORD hears, and delivers them out of all their troubles.

During their captivity, Nebuchadnezzar, king of Babylon, decreed that no one could ask any petition of any god or man for thirty days. Daniel, a Hebrew in Babylon (today's Iraq) and a man of great faith and integrity, refused to obey the decree of the king. He continued to pray three times each day (Daniel 6:1-23), just as he had done prior to the king's decree. Daniel honored God; and when his worship led to his being thrown into a den of lions, God responded by shutting the mouths of the beasts. Daniel's prayers prevailed in the midst of Israel's captivity:

> For thus says the Lord: After seventy years are completed at Babylon, I will visit you and perform My good word toward you, and cause you to return to this place. For I know the thoughts that I think toward you, says the Lord, thoughts of peace and not of evil, to give you a future and a hope. Then you will call upon Me and go and pray to Me, and I will listen to you. And you will seek Me and find Me, when you search for Me with all your heart. I will be found by you, says the Lord, and I will bring you back from your captivity; I will gather you from all the nations and from all the places where I have driven you, says the Lord, and I will bring you to the place from which I cause you to be carried away captive. —Jeremiah 29:10–14

Darkness flees when we pray! Demons tremble when we pray. Heaven moves when we pray, and angels receive assignments when we pray. Prayer affects three realms: the divine, the angelic, and the human. Without it, demons rule uncontested.

The apostle Paul wrote to the Ephesians in chapter 6, verses 10–18a:

> Finally, my brethren, be strong in the Lord and in the power of His might. Put on the whole armor of God, that

you may be able to stand against the wiles of the devil. For we do not wrestle against flesh and blood, but against principalities, against powers, against the rulers of the darkness of this age, against spiritual hosts of wickedness in the heavenly places. Therefore take up the whole armor of God, that you may be able to withstand in the evil day, and having done all, to stand. Stand therefore, having girded your waist with truth, having put on the breastplate of righteousness, and having shod your feet with the preparation of the gospel of peace; above all, taking the shield of faith with which you will be able to quench all the fiery darts of the wicked one. And take the helmet of salvation, and the sword of the Spirit, which is the word of God; praying always with all prayer and supplication in the Spirit . . .

Believers are often engaged in a sober spiritual struggle. If we as watchmen refuse or fail to take our place on the wall, the consequences can be deadly. Vigilance is the key; apathy is destructive. You and I have the God-given responsibility to watch and pray.

In 1 Thessalonians 5:17, Paul writes that we are to "pray without ceasing" (KJV). He is, quite obviously, not telling us to stay on our knees in a posture of prayer twenty-four hours each day. That would be nearly impossible. His admonition refers to a mindset of always being conscious of our heavenly Father and living a life of surrender to Him and His will. It is an awareness of the truth that God should govern our every thought and action.

One writer proffered this advice:

> When our thoughts turn to worry, fear, discouragement, and anger, we are to consciously and quickly turn every thought into prayer and every prayer into thanksgiving. In his letter to the Philippians, Paul commands us to stop being anxious and instead, "in everything, by prayer and petition, with thanksgiving, present your requests to God" (Philippians 4:6). He taught the believers at Colossae to devote themselves "to prayer, being watchful and thankful" (Colossians 4:2). Paul exhorted the Ephesian believers to see prayer as a weapon to use in fighting spiritual battles (Ephesians 6:18). As we go through the day, prayer should be our first response to every fearful situation, every anxious thought, and every undesired task that God commands. A lack of prayer will cause us to depend on ourselves instead of depending on God's grace.

To pray without ceasing is to reveal our total reliance on and dependence upon our profound relationship with our Father God.

*The Lord has heard my plea;
the Lord accepts my prayer.*

—PSALM 6:9 ESV

Prayer is as essential as air and water if we are to maintain a spiritual life of constant contact with God. If we don't make that connection, no matter how sincere our intentions, we will not see a change in the circumstances of our life. We must pray! James 4:2 tells us:

> You lust and do not have. You murder and covet and cannot obtain. You fight and war. *Yet you do not have because you do not ask* (emphasis mine).

During a dark hour of Israel's history, the Assyrians demanded heavy tribute from King Hezekiah. In response, Hezekiah stripped the temple of its gold and silver in order to meet that demand. Still, that was not enough; the Assyrians mounted an attack against the city. When King Hezekiah was informed in a letter from the king of

Assyria that Israel would be destroyed if the demands were not met, he took the letter to the temple. There, in the presence of God, he spread the letter on the altar and prayed:

> O Lord God of Israel, the One who dwells between the cherubim, You are God, You alone, of all the kingdoms of the earth. You have made heaven and earth. Incline Your ear, O Lord, and hear; open Your eyes, O Lord, and see; and hear the words of Sennacherib, which he has sent to reproach the living God. . . . Now therefore, O Lord our God, I pray, save us from his hand, that all the kingdoms of the earth may know that You are the Lord God, You alone. —2 Kings 19:15–16, 19

God answered the king's prayer with an overwhelming victory! The Bible says the angel of the Lord killed 185,000 Assyrian soldiers in one night. In great gratitude for God's mercy, Hezekiah cleansed, repaired, and reopened the temple of God. Worship to Jehovah was restored, daily sacrifices were resumed, and the Passover Feast was again celebrated by the nation of Israel.

Years earlier, when King Solomon had prayed at the dedication of the temple, God revealed himself and His plan to Solomon with great power:

> Then the Lord appeared to Solomon by night, and said to him: "I have heard your prayer, and have chosen

this place for Myself as a house of sacrifice. When I shut up heaven and there is no rain, or command the locusts to devour the land, or send pestilence among My people, if My people who are called by My name will humble themselves, and pray and seek My face, and turn from their wicked ways, then I will hear from heaven, and will forgive their sin and heal their land. Now My eyes will be open and My ears attentive to prayer made in this place. For now I have chosen and sanctified this house, that My name may be there forever; and My eyes and My heart will be there perpetually." —2 Chronicles 7:12–16

Isaiah encouraged the Israelites with: "Then you shall call, and the LORD will answer; you shall cry, and He will say, 'Here I am'" (Isaiah 58:9).

King Solomon prophesied that a national revival would come to Israel. It has yet to occur, but when that renewal does come, it will certainly be through the power of prayer. You and I can help usher in that renewal through prayer. While the world attempts to find an answer to the continuing crisis in the Middle East by political means, you and I have the key in our hands: prayer. That is but one of the reasons the apostle Paul admonished believers to "pray without ceasing" (1 Thessalonians 5:17 KJV).

Perhaps you might be compared to Jonah; he did everything *but* pray. God had given him specific instructions in chapter one, verses 1–2:

> Now the word of the LORD came to Jonah the son of Amittai, saying, "Arise, go to Nineveh, that great city, and cry out against it; for their wickedness has come up before Me."

Jonah knew what he was supposed to do:

> But Jonah arose to flee to Tarshish from the presence of the LORD. He went down to Joppa, and found a ship going to Tarshish; so he paid the fare, and went down into it, to go with them to Tarshish from the presence of the LORD. —Jonah 1:3

Rather than acquiesce to the voice of Jehovah, Jonah fled and ended up in the belly of a big fish, one especially prepared by God to mete out correction. There, churning around in the contents of the stomach of God's creation, the prophet cried out to Jehovah, against whom he had sinned. God intervened and caused the fish to vomit Jonah out onto dry land. Even the fish of the sea are subject to the power of answered prayer. What a sight that must have been! When those in Nineveh saw this reeking, rancid, bedraggled prophet stagger into town, they must first have been disinclined to even get close enough to hear his message. However, once they began to hear of coming annihilation, they heeded, repented quickly, and then God sent the promised revival.

In Revelation 8:3–5, the apostle John is shown the power of prayer:

> Then another angel, having a golden censer, came and stood at the altar. He was given much incense, that he should offer it with the prayers of all the saints upon the golden altar which was before the throne. And the smoke of the incense, with the prayers of the saints, ascended before God from the angel's hand. Then the angel took the censer, filled it with fire from the altar, and threw it to the earth. And there were noises, thunderings, lightnings, and an earthquake.

In light of what we have discovered about the efficacy of prayer, two of the saddest scriptures in the Bible can be found in Ezekiel and Isaiah:

> So I sought for a man among them who would make a wall, and stand in the gap before Me on behalf of the land, that I should not destroy it; but I found no one.
> —Ezekiel 22:30

> He [God] saw that there was no man, and wondered that there was no intercessor. —Isaiah 59:16

No one to stand in the gap. No one to intercede. What a tragic picture! Today, God is still looking for that man, woman, young person, or child who will commit to stand in the breach and pray. Will you, like Isaiah, say, "Here am I! Send me" (Isaiah 6:8)?

The children of Israel sinned in the wilderness, fashioning a golden calf, dancing before it, and denying God's sovereignty, and God threatened to destroy them:

> Now when the people saw that Moses delayed coming down from the mountain, the people gathered together to Aaron, and said to him, "Come, make us gods that shall go before us; for as for this Moses, the man who brought us up out of the land of Egypt, we do not know what has become of him." And Aaron said to them, "Break off the golden earrings which are in the ears of your wives, your sons, and your daughters, and bring them to me." So all the people broke off the golden earrings which were in their ears, and brought them to Aaron. And he received the gold from their hand, and he fashioned it with an engraving tool, and made a molded calf.... And the Lord said to Moses, "I have seen this people, and indeed it is a stiff-necked people! Now therefore, let Me alone, that My wrath may burn hot against them and I may consume them. And I will make of you a great nation." —Exodus 32:1–4, 9–10

Moses fell on his face before Jehovah God. The psalmist wrote in Psalm 106:23:

> Therefore He said that He would destroy them,

had not Moses His chosen one stood before Him in the breach, to turn away His wrath, lest He destroy them.

The time has come for Christians everywhere to stand up and "Blow the trumpet in Zion, consecrate a fast, call a sacred assembly" (Joel 2:15). There is a gap, a breach to be filled, and a price to be paid. Dedicated watchmen are needed on every wall. God's Word is rife with examples of intercessors who prevailed against the enemy, the prayer warriors of Hebrews 11 who subdued kingdoms, shut the mouths of lions, set armies to flight, raised the dead, and secured the promises of God—all through faith in God and prayer!

Daniel put his life on the line by praying three times a day despite the king's order to abstain. Prayer is a priority we cannot and must not overlook. Israel's, and indeed America's, future hope lies in the hands of prayer warriors, those who will take up the banner and commit to prayer. It is not the last resort; it is the *first step* in winning the battle against the evil that stalks this world today.

If Daniel prayed and mighty angels were sent to do battle against demon spirits, so can you and I. Since Daniel lived in the Babylonian Empire, it is quite possible that the prince of Persia he fought in the spirit was one of the same spirits at work today to bring death and destruction. Regardless of which spirits are now involved or how many there are, the clarion call goes out to God-fearing people everywhere to man the battle stations and fight the war in prayer.

Just as America has been forced to take the war on terrorism to the battlefields of the nations that sponsor it, we must take our fight to the battlefield in the spiritual realm to defeat the demons that sponsor it. We must take the battle to the enemy and defeat them through prayer in the name of Jesus!

Prayer is the only exploit that takes hold of eternity. It is the action that touches heaven, and moves earth. It pierces the heart of God, turns the head of God, and moves the hand of God. For a Christian, it is not the last resort . . . it must always be the first line of defense!

Through prayer, we must do everything possible to overthrow kingdoms of darkness, shut the mouths of the lions of terror, and quench the flames of hell by the power of almighty God! How you and I respond to God's call will determine whether we succeed or fail. The people of God have been called to intercede for and to comfort the Jewish people. Will you accept the call?

Moses stood between the avenging angel and the children of Israel in the desert; Ruth stood beside Naomi and cared for her; Esther stood beside Mordecai and risked her life for her people; and Nehemiah stood upon the walls of Jerusalem and directed its reconstruction while armed for battle. It is time for the church to remain firm in support of Israel.

In Joel 2:17, we are admonished:

Let the priests, who minister to the LORD, weep between the porch and the altar; let them say, "Spare Your people, O LORD, and do not give Your heritage to reproach, that the nations should rule over them. Why should they say among the peoples, 'Where is their God?'" Joel 2:17

The merciful are honored by God: "He who oppresses the poor reproaches his Maker, but he who honors Him has mercy on the needy" (Proverbs 14:31).

If Christians who are able to bless the house of Israel withhold that encouragement, especially by not reaching out to those who are suffering from terrorist attacks, how will the Jewish people ever know that real Christians are different from those who call themselves Christians but kill His people? To comfort the house of Israel is our duty and our privilege. Jesus was compassion personified: "But when He saw the multitudes, He was moved with compassion for them, because they were weary and scattered, like sheep having no shepherd" (Matthew 9:36).

God has always sought volunteers to pray, to speak, and to perform His work on Earth with love and compassion. The story of Isaiah is a perfect example: King Uzziah had been a good king, a rare leader of God's people, and Isaiah was heartbroken when he died. It was at this time that God comforted Isaiah by showing him that the King of Kings was still on the throne:

> In the year that King Uzziah died, I saw the Lord sitting on a throne, high and lifted up, and the train of His robe filled the temple. —Isaiah 6:1

When Isaiah realized that Jehovah God was still in control, when he glimpsed the One whose throne is elevated above every other, and who was still in charge, Isaiah was awed by the holiness of God and convicted of his own uncleanness. He fell on his face, repented, and the angel cleansed him of his iniquity.

> Then one of the seraphim flew to me, having in his hand a live coal which he had taken with the tongs from the altar. And he touched my mouth with it, and said:
>
> "Behold, this has touched your lips; your iniquity is taken away, and your sin purged." —Isaiah 6:6–7

The prophet was cleansed of his iniquity. Then Isaiah was ready for his commission. Are you?

I heard the voice of the Lord, saying:

> "Whom shall I send, and who will go for Us?"
> Then I said, "Here am I! Send me." —Isaiah 6:8

Be advised of this one thing: Prayer is costly. Author Paul Lee Tan recorded the following admonition:

"I want you to spend fifteen minutes every day praying for foreign missions," said a pastor to some young people in his congregation. . . .

"Be sure it is a dangerous thing to pray in earnest for this work; you will find that you cannot pray and withhold your labour, or pray and withhold your money; indeed, you will no longer be your own when your prayers begin to be answered."

4

Eli responded, "Go in peace, and may the God of Israel grant the request you've made of him."

—1 Samuel 1:17 csb

Hannah, wife of Elkanah, a Kohathite of the tribe of Levi, must have felt a great sense of despair when, month after month, she remained barren. Hannah might have felt that by not bearing a child with Elkanah she lacked status and merit in his eyes. Author and professor Dr. Noreen Jacks wrote of the stigma of barrenness:

> Barren women were habitually taunted and ridiculed, made to feel like second class citizens, and were considered a public embarrassment to their husbands. The shame of barrenness was always on the minds of infertile couples. In some societies, husbands were free to acquire secondary wives or concubines to fulfill their need for progeny, preferably a male heir. The childless

couple faced an uncertain future with no offspring to work the fields, tend the herds, and assist with the daily chores in the home. Even worse, who would care for the couple in old age, mourn their passing, bury them with dignity, memorialize them annually, and carry the family name to the next generation and beyond? Such were the time-honored duties of one's loyal children. With critical needs of this magnitude, it is not surprising that desperate people in the ancient world were obsessed with reproduction of the species.

It must have been emotionally draining for both Hannah and her husband that she had failed to present him with a child from their union.

Being from the tribe of Levi, Elkanah was likely among those responsible for leading praise and worship in the tabernacle at Shiloh. Each year he was summoned for several weeks to serve Jehovah. As a faithful and devout wife, Hannah often accompanied him. While Elkanah fulfilled his duties in the tabernacle, Hannah would slip away to a quiet place in the tabernacle to petition for Jehovah's favor and for an end to her infertility.

One day as she prayed fervently, she was in such despair that her lips moved silently as tears rained unchecked down her cheeks. Only a barren woman can totally understand Hannah's sense of frustration and unhappiness and her petition for a son in 1 Samuel 1:11. James, in chapter 5 verse 16, would perhaps call Hannah's prayer of despair a "fervent and effectual prayer." When Eli, the high priest, saw her he came to the erroneous conclusion that the woman was drunk and had no place in the vicinity of the tabernacle. He marched over to where Hannah bowed beneath her burden of hopelessness, reprimanded her, and then shamed her drunken state. Aghast at his rebuke, Hannah responded:

> No, my lord, I am a woman troubled in spirit. I have drunk neither wine nor strong drink, but I have been pouring out my soul before the LORD.—1 Samuel 1:15 ESV

Eli then blessed her and sent her on her way with the inexplicable sense of peace and hope that Jehovah had heard her prayer. Assuredly He had; soon Hannah was able to reveal to Elkanah that she was with child, and not many months later, she presented Elkanah with a child that she had named Samuel (which means "God heard").

During her prayer in the tabernacle, Hannah had made a vow to Jehovah:

> O LORD of hosts, if you will indeed look on the affliction of your servant and remember me and not forget your servant, but will give to your servant a son, then I will give him to the LORD all the days of his life, and no razor shall touch his head. —1 Samuel 1:11 ESV

Just as she had promised, when the child was weaned, Hannah took him with her to the tabernacle in Shiloh and presented him to Eli so Samuel could be instructed in the ways of the Lord. Each year thereafter, she would make a new robe for her son and take it to him.

According to *Easton's Bible Dictionary*, the gift was not just an article of clothing but rather had special significance:

> And each year, when they came up to Shiloh, Hannah brought to her absent child "a little coat" (Heb. meil, a term used to denote the "robe" of the ephod worn by the high priest, (Exodus 28:31), a priestly robe, a long upper tunic (I Chronicles 15:27), in which to minister in the tabernacle (I Samuel 2:19; 15:27; Job 2:12).

Hannah's prayer of despair was answered in a miraculous way that brought about the birth of Samuel, who would grow up to be a great prophet in Israel. He, in turn, would anoint a shepherd boy named David to become king and establish Jerusalem as his capital city. It was this same David who would write, "Morning, noon, and night I cry out in my distress, and the LORD hears my voice" (Psalm 55:17 NLT).

My wife, Carolyn, taught me a faith lesson when our fourth and last child was born. I had secretly wanted a son to love, probably because I never had a father who loved *me*. I thought I would only have my three beautiful daughters, which was fine with me; they are my sweethearts! But God gave Carolyn and me another child.

Carolyn obstinately refused to listen to the opinions of others—those who told her she would have another girl. She believed God had told her a boy was on the way. Her belief persisted even after the doctor announced that she would have another girl. Let me repeat that: She believed God! She was totally convinced—against all odds—that our baby would be a boy and declared that he would be named Michael David Evans II. I reminded Carolyn that I didn't have a middle name. Of course, it didn't faze her at all; the new mother won that battle. Soon after our son's birth, I appeared before a judge to have my name changed to Michael David Evans. Both my son and I are now named "David" as are hundreds and thousands of boys and their fathers worldwide. Michael David has grown up to be a godly man of integrity. I have told him, "I was named after you. When I grow up, I want to be just like you."

Hannah's miracle son, Samuel, had grown up to be a man of integrity and prayer. He stood before the people of Israel on one occasion and said, "Far be it from me that I should sin against the LORD in ceasing to pray for you" (1 Samuel 12:23). Samuel grew up to be more than simply an answer to prayer; he became a priest, judge, and prophet who later anointed both Saul and David as kings over Judah.

There were other men and women in the Bible who cried out in despair only to have God hear and answer their prayers; the most notable was our Lord. Following His triumphal entry into Jerusalem, Jesus and his disciples gathered to celebrate Passover. As the observance drew to a close the group arose from the table and made their way to the garden of Gethsemane. With foreknowledge of the events that were about to culminate in His death, Jesus likely felt an overwhelming need to talk with His heavenly Father. He stationed the disciples a short distance away. Jesus walked farther into the garden and fell on His face in prayer and supplication. Perhaps it was there in the garden that Jesus really understood the abhorrence of the task that confronted Him. He would certainly have read the words of Isaiah the prophet in chapter 53, verses 4–10. Again, *The Message* gives these verses such a graphic quality:

> But the fact is, it was *our* pains he carried—*our* disfigurements, all the things wrong with *us*. We thought he brought it on himself, that God was punishing him for his own failures. But it was our sins that did that to him, that ripped and tore and crushed him—*our sins!* He took the punishment, and that made us whole. Through his bruises we get healed. We're all like sheep who've wandered off and gotten lost. We've all done our own thing, gone our own way. And GOD has piled all our sins, everything we've done wrong, on him, on him. He was beaten, he was tortured, but he didn't say a word. Like a lamb taken to be slaughtered and like a sheep being sheared, he took it all in silence. Justice miscarried, and he was led off—and did anyone really know what was happening? He died without a thought for his own

welfare, beaten bloody for the sins of my people. They buried him with the wicked, threw him in a grave with a rich man, even though he'd never hurt a soul or said one word that wasn't true. Still, it's what GOD had in mind all along, to crush him with pain. The plan was that he give himself as an offering for sin so that he'd see life come from it—life, life, and more life. And GOD's plan will deeply prosper through him.

There in the garden of Gethsemane, it all came flooding in—what He, the Son of Man, must endure, how He must die, the degradation and pain of crucifixion—and it was overwhelming. Luke paints the picture of Jesus' despair and travail as He prayed the prayer that never fails:

And He was withdrawn from them about a stone's throw, and He knelt down and prayed, saying, "Father, if it is Your will, take this cup away from Me; *nevertheless not My will, but Yours, be done.*" Then an angel appeared to Him from heaven, strengthening Him. And being in agony, He prayed more earnestly. Then His sweat became like great drops of blood falling down to the ground. —Luke 22:41-44 (emphasis mine)

It is at this point, I believe, the knowledge that He was to be the sacrificial Lamb must have hit like the force of a huge boulder rolling downhill and slamming into the valley below. He, Jesus of Nazareth, was the "Lamb slain from the foundation of the world" (Revelation 13:8 KJV).

Perhaps it was then that His "sweat was as it were great drops of blood falling down to the ground" (Luke 22:44 KJV). Was it here that He began to feel the burden of the sins of all mankind descending on His sinless shoulders—lust, greed, wrath, pride, envy, sloth, gluttony? Figuratively, He was about to become a murderer, thief, rapist, terrorist, prostitute, wife beater, pedophile, or any of the other heinous crimes daily perpetrated against humanity. He who knew no sin was heaped with the sins of the world, and about to be betrayed into the hands of His accusers. There in Gethsemane, He was served a foretaste of what would happen the following day.

The Son of Man was so overcome by the magnitude of what He was about to face that He prayed in desperation. Jesus was staggered by the bitterness of the cup He had been asked to drink, at the cross He had been asked to shoulder, and yet He just as desperately wanted to do the Father's will. He desired *that* more than He valued His own life. Jesus was about to be crushed by the weight of sin just as the fruit of the olive tree was crushed by the stone press. Pressed from our Savior was not oil but rather a perfect plan for our salvation fueled by a love that will not let us go.

The answer to Jesus' prayer of despair was the salvation of mankind. Jesus offered one sacrifice: Himself. He established the plan of forgiveness and reconciliation one time for all time! He had laid aside His robes of glory and donned a robe of flesh so that we might have access to God, the Father. We read in 2 Corinthians 5:21, "For our sake he made him to be sin who knew no sin, so that in him we might become the righteousness of God" (ESV).

Blood-bought, forgiven, redeemed, and delivered! Believers are not saved by the *character* of the sacrifice; salvation only comes through the shed blood of Christ—the faultless, flawless, and final price of atonement.

5

*But now, O Lord, You are our Father,
we are the clay, and You our potter;
and all of us are the work of Your hand.*

—ISAIAH 64:8 NASB

In 1963 when I was sixteen, my family still lived at 77 Pasco Road in the Indian Orchard neighborhood of Springfield, Massachusetts. I knew I had to find a way out of my father's house. As with most Americans, the Evans family was in shock over the assassination of President John F. Kennedy on November 22 of that year. The legendary Kennedy family was from New England, as was I, and on that fateful day, I decided to join the army to defend my country.

I had lived under the verbal and physical assault meted out by my father as long as I could. As I got older, the physical abuse had lessened, but the verbal abuse never abated. A constant barrage of put-downs and slurs followed me, usually beginning with Dad's favorite: "Moron." A war somewhere, anywhere, in the world looked like the best opportunity to escape the unceasing battles at home, and with things heating up in Vietnam and US troops still subject to skirmishes in Korea, the time seemed right. I gathered my courage and determination and made my way down to the local army recruiter's office to enlist. Somehow I passed the written test but then flunked the physical. I was already tall for my age but thin as a rail at 111 pounds.

Undeterred, I continued to pursue ways to achieve my lifelong dream of running as far away from my father as I could get. My buddy Jim helped me formulate a plan that would make me seem heavier than I really was. That was coupled with the recruiter's off-the-wall suggestion that I eat bananas—lots of bananas. When I returned to the recruiting office later, I had secreted four five-pound rubber weights that I had purchased at Ryan's Sporting Goods. They were attached to my body by two stretch belts wound around each thigh, high under the legs of my boxers. When the recruiter asked me to strip down to my shorts, I did, and then took tiny steps, worrying with each one that the weights were going to shift. And shift they did! I fell to my knees in pain and despair, fighting back the tears that threatened. Unbelievably, no one seemed to notice as I slowly stood and cautiously made my way to the scale.

The sergeant smiled and said, "Boy, I can't believe it. You're in, but you're still too young; you've got to be seventeen and have your parents' permission. Come back on your seventeenth birthday and we'll swear you in then. You'll be in the army." I was going to be in the army! It was one of the proudest days of my life. The sergeant continued, "Now, before you leave, tell me: Do you have any idea where you'd like to be stationed?" I looked on the map that was posted on the wall of the recruiter's office and tried to find the farthest place from 77 Pasco Road. There were pushpins to indicate where US military troops were stationed. There it was! A tiny pink messed-up rectangle: Korea. Although the Korean War had officially ended in 1953, the United States still had troops stationed in South Korea along the demilitarized zone to deter the North Koreans from slipping across the border. That's where I wanted to go.

After my birthday, and with my father's written permission in hand, I was sworn in and then sent to boot camp. After graduation, I was shipped off to spend fourteen months in East Asia on a mountain the Koreans called Wong Tong Nee. Early one morning as I wandered around the mountain, not even thinking about God or my encounter with Jesus all those years earlier, I felt something I had not felt since He had visited me—the overwhelming presence of God settling over me. Joy unspeakable and full of glory filled my soul. Like Samuel of old, my spirit whispered, *Speak, Lord, for thy servant heareth* (1 Samuel 3:10). All too often our prayer is, "Listen, Lord, don't you know *I'm* talking to You?" It is infinitely more important that *we* listen!

Finding a secluded spot, I sank to the ground and tears streamed down my face as Jesus gently reminded my spirit of His words to me when I was eleven. I whispered, "Will you ever talk to me again? I need to hear Your voice. I sense the same presence I did when I was eleven." He did not answer me audibly, but suddenly I felt impressed by the Holy Spirit to turn to Daniel 10:9–11. With tears misting my eyes, I pulled my Bible from my backpack and read:

> Yet I heard the sound of his words; and while I heard the sound of his words I was in a deep sleep on my face, with my face to the ground. Suddenly, a hand touched me, which made me tremble on my knees and on the palms of my hands. And he said to me, "O Daniel, man greatly beloved, understand the words that I speak to you, and stand upright, for I have now been sent to you."

As the Holy Spirit spoke these words to me, I stood trembling and weeping. Eventually, the sensation of God's presence lifted, but I possessed a newfound sense of peace. I realized then that I was *eager* to hear the voice of God again. I *needed* to hear His voice—it gave me the affirmation I desperately needed to overcome. It also gave me the divine direction I craved. I had not heard His voice for nearly nine years. The Spirit of God I had just experienced on Wong Tong Nee was the same presence I had encountered in my bedroom—first the presence, then the voice. Now I had experienced His presence, but where was His voice?

Before leaving the spot that day, I gathered twelve stones and set up a small altar. Sometime during the day, every day, I returned to that spot to pray and seek God. During the monsoon season when the rains came, I could be found wrapped in my rubber poncho praying by my rock altar. In the middle of the blistering summer, with temperatures rising above 110 degrees, I would pray in the shade of those rocks. In the frigid winter, when the chill factor dropped to 20 degrees below zero, I would wrap myself in layers of clothing and go to pray at my altar of rocks. As I studied the Scriptures, I discovered that God did, indeed, have a divine plan for my life. I was His son, and He loved me.

Years later I returned to South Korea with Dr. Bill Bright, founder of Campus Crusade for Christ. It was then I discovered that after I had fulfilled my military obligation and gone home, Dr. Paul Cho purchased the mountain and made it a place of prayer, which came to be called simply "Prayer Mountain." During that trip Dr. Cho said to me, "You were the first Christian to pray atop the mountain." He called me "Holy Ghost Kimchi Man, Seed of Abraham." I know now that God wanted me to learn to pray, learn to listen to Him, and learn how to seek His will and plan for my life atop that lonely mountain. I knew that a plan had been established for me; I just needed to know how to allow God to unlock His purpose in my life.

On that mountain in South Korea as I studied the book of Daniel, I began to see it as more than a treatise on the end times. It is also an in-depth study on consecration, dedication, integrity, and sanctification.

Daniel and three young companions were among the scores carried off to Babylon by Nebuchadnezzar's armies. They were snatched from their homes and families, and we are not told if any family members survived the battle and ransacking of Jerusalem. The young men would be forced to endure whatever trials and degradation faced them. Despite the circumstances surrounding these four young men, they did not relinquish their faith in Jehovah.

These Hebrew boys from noble, nurturing families had been accustomed to being in a warm and caring atmosphere. They were homesick and unsettled, and things would only get worse. Their familial protection had been stripped from them, and they were at the mercy of a pagan king and his minions. Yet God had not forsaken them; their training had not abandoned them; their faith in Jehovah was secure. They would be faced with trials and demands that would challenge their beliefs—would they remain faithful?

One of the first tests to which Daniel, Shadrach, Meshach, and Abednego would be subjected was over the food provided to them. The king had ordered that they be fed from his table:

> Then the king ordered Ashpenaz, chief of his court officials, to bring into the king's service some of the Israelites from the royal family and the nobility—young men without any physical defect, handsome, showing aptitude for every kind of learning, well informed, quick to understand, and qualified to serve in the king's palace. He was to teach them the language and literature of the Babylonians. The king assigned them a daily amount of food and wine from the king's table. They were to be trained for three years, and after that they were to enter the king's service. Among those who were chosen were

some from Judah: Daniel, Hananiah, Mishael and Azariah. The chief official gave them new names: to Daniel, the name Belteshazzar; to Hananiah, Shadrach; to Mishael, Meshach; and to Azariah, Abednego. —Daniel 1:3–7 NIV

The three young men were determined not to eat the food offered to idols, and petitioned the Babylonian official to allow them to partake of only vegetables and water. With reluctance, the keeper agreed. The resolve of the young men and their obedience to God's law won them the respect of the official, of Nebuchadnezzar, and of God. They had passed the first test with flying colors, but a more difficult test lurked around the corner. How would they handle a life-threatening situation?

Nebuchadnezzar was not unlike many in the public eye today: He began to believe his own hype, his own public relations fantasies. As his ego grew, so did his desire to erect a statue that would reflect his untold wealth and power. His artisans loosely based the design of the image on a dream that Nebuchadnezzar had experienced, the meaning of which Daniel had interpreted. The king opened the doors to his vast storehouses of golden treasure to provide the materials from which the idol was to be made. It is entirely possible that some of the golden vessels taken from the temple in Jerusalem were included in those melted and used to fashion the commanded graven image.

The Chaldeans worshiped a number of heathen deities, but

nothing as brilliant and magnificent as the statue that rose up from the plain of Dura. It was said to be ninety feet tall and nine feet wide—probably with an appearance much like an obelisk. Nebuchadnezzar was elated with the statue when it was completed and issued an edict to the people of Babylon: The graven image was to be dedicated as an object of worship, and all would display their consummate devotion by bowing down before the idol:

> As soon as you hear the sound of the horn, flute, zither, lyre, harp, pipe and all kinds of music, you must fall down and worship the image of gold that King Nebuchadnezzar has set up. Whoever does not fall down and worship will immediately be thrown into a blazing furnace. —Daniel 3:5–6 NIV

Now, Daniel and his friends had cut their teeth on the laws of God, specifically the Ten Commandments. These edicts were woven into the very fabric of their lives. Moses had instructed the children of Israel in Deuteronomy 11:19 that the Word of Jehovah was to be taught to the children "when you sit in your house, when you walk by the way, when you lie down, and when you rise up." The tenets and precepts of God's law were deeply ingrained in the minds and spirits of those young men.

The first and second commandments are very specific:

> You shall have no other gods before me. You shall

not make for yourself an image in the form of anything in heaven above or on the earth beneath or in the waters below. You shall not bow down to them or worship them.
—Exodus 20:3–5a NIV

The day appointed by Nebuchadnezzar arrived, accompanied by great pomp and ceremony. Off to one side of the dais from which the king held court was a reminder of the punishment for disobedience: the ovens into which those who refused to bow would be thrown. (It is possible that those very ovens were used to smelt the ore or melt the gold used to fashion the giant idol.) On the plain surrounding the image, his subjects gathered awaiting the strains of musical instruments that were to signal the moment to fall on their faces and worship the golden statue.

The demons of darkness must have danced in anticipation of the destruction of that trio of Hebrews in the king's court—those who were likely to refuse the order to bow. Satan probably waited with sulfurous breath to see the defeat this trio of God's chosen children. The king had decreed compliance with his edict; God declared a different scenario, one that would leave the ruler appalled and astounded. When Nebuchadnezzar's watchmen looked out over the prostrate participants, they saw three young men standing tall—Shadrach, Meshach, and Abednego. The Hebrews were determined not to disgrace the God of heaven. Jehovah was their Lord and King—they would bow to no other. Their detractors—those jealous of the honors that had been bestowed on Daniel and his companions—could not wait to advise the king that three of his subjects had dared to flagrantly defy his order:

> But there are some Jews whom you have set over the affairs of the province of Babylon—Shadrach, Meshach and Abednego—who pay no attention to you, Your Majesty. They neither serve your gods nor worship the image of gold you have set up. —Daniel 3:12 NIV

Nebuchadnezzar's anger erupted. How dare they disobey his commandment! He ordered the men brought to stand before him. He demanded, "Is it true? Did you not bow down before the golden image as I ordered? Don't you know the punishment that awaits you if you refuse to bow?"

Shadrach, Meshach, and Abednego quietly explained to the king that they could not bow to any image because of their fidelity to Jehovah God. Nebuchadnezzar's visage grew darker as he pointed toward the ovens burning brightly in the distance—a visible reminder of his edict. He ordered the musicians to play again to give these three young men a second chance to adhere to his instructions. Again they refused. As they stood before the king, the three Hebrew men replied:

> King Nebuchadnezzar, we do not need to defend ourselves before you in this matter. If we are thrown into

the blazing furnace, the God we serve is able to deliver us from it, and he will deliver us from Your Majesty's hand. But even if he does not, we want you to know, Your Majesty, that we will not serve your gods or worship the image of gold you have set up. —Daniel 3:16–18 NIV

The king was further infuriated by their answer—the heat of his anger perhaps rivaling the heat of the ovens. He ordered the furnaces stoked seven times hotter. He then commanded the mightiest soldiers in his army to bind the three men and toss them into the fire. So hot was the inferno that the men who marched Shadrach, Meshach, and Abednego to the furnace were burned alive. The path forward was desolate, dim, and desperate—"But God," (Don't you love those two words?). *But God* had neither forgotten nor overlooked the dedication of His children determined to do His will. *But God* gives life instead of death. *But God* gives grace instead of cruel punishment. *But God* rescues instead of abandoning us to destruction.

As the men who stood strong in His Name landed in the midst of the fire, He poured out His favor upon them and joined them there. As the fire lapped up the bindings of His servants, Jehovah tamed the flames, which lost their ability to devour.

From his royal perch high above the furnace, the king watched in anticipation of seeing the three defiant Hebrews totally incinerated. Suddenly, his triumph turned to fear. He grew pale as he lurched from the throne and pointed toward the all-consuming flames.

He stuttered, "Did we not cast three men bound into the midst of the fire? . . . Look! . . . I see four men loose, walking in the midst of the fire; and they are not hurt, and the form of the fourth is like the Son of God" (Daniel 3:24–25).

Arthur Smith wrote a rousing spiritual about the experiences of the three Hebrew children titled "The Fourth Man." The chorus reads:

> They wouldn't bend
> They held onto the will of God so we are told
> They wouldn't bow
> They would not bow their knees to the idol made of gold
> They wouldn't burn
> They were protected by the fourth man in the fire
> They wouldn't bend, they wouldn't bow
> They wouldn't burn.

In amazement, the king abandoned his throne and strode across the plain. He crept as close to the fire as he safely could and cried:

> "Shadrach, Meshach and Abed-Nego, servants of the Most High God, come out, and come here." Then Shadrach, Meshach, and Abed-Nego came from the midst of the fire. And the satraps, administrators, governors, and the king's counselors gathered together, and they saw these men on whose bodies the fire had no

power; the hair of their head was not singed nor were their garments affected, and the smell of fire was not on them. —Daniel 3:26–27

Nebuchadnezzar was overwhelmed by the miracle that accompanied the obedience of the three men to the Most High God. He decreed:

"Blessed be the God of Shadrach, Meshach, and Abed-Nego, who sent His Angel and delivered His servants who trusted in Him, and they have frustrated the king's word, and yielded their bodies, that they should not serve nor worship any god except their own God! Therefore I make a decree that any people, nation, or language which speaks anything amiss against the God of Shadrach, Meshach, and Abed-Nego shall be cut in pieces, and their houses shall be made an ash heap; because there is no other God who can deliver like this." Then the king promoted Shadrach, Meshach, and Abed-Nego in the province of Babylon. —Daniel 3:28–30

Consecration to God won the favor of the king and of Jehovah, who honored their faithfulness.

6

And everyone who calls on the name of the Lord will be saved;
for on Mount Zion and in Jerusalem there will be deliverance,
as the LORD has said, even among the survivors whom the LORD calls.

—JOEL 2:32 NIV

There would also be a test of obedience for Daniel just as life threatening as the one had been for his friends Shadrach, Meshach, and Abednego. In chapter 5 of Daniel, Babylon fell to the Medes and Persians. Three major prophets—Isaiah, Jeremiah, and Daniel—had each prophesied that Nebuchadnezzar's kingdom would fall:

> Behold, I will stir up the Medes against them, who will not regard silver; and as for gold, they will not delight in it. Also their bows will dash the young men to pieces, and they will have no pity on the fruit of the womb; their eye will not spare children. —Isaiah 13:17–18

Jeremiah foretold the reason for the rise of the Medes and Persians and the reason for the invasion:

> The LORD has raised up the spirit of the kings of the Medes. For His plan is against Babylon to destroy it, because it is the vengeance of the LORD, the vengeance for His temple. —Jeremiah 51:11

> "And I will repay Babylon and all the inhabitants of Chaldea for all the evil they have done in Zion in your sight," says the LORD. —Jeremiah 51:24

The hordes took the entire kingdom from Nebuchadnezzar without having so much as launched an arrow or raised a lance. The prophet Isaiah cried: "Babylon is fallen, is fallen! And all the carved images of her gods He has broken to the ground" (Isaiah 21:9).

Nebuchadnezzar's golden idols had been crushed into dust.

The amazing thing about the bloodless coup was how little it affected Daniel's position in the king's court. He survived the upheaval, and at the beginning of chapter 5 we read that he was appointed as one of three governors over the kingdom. The new king was Darius, who ruled contemporaneously with Cyrus.

One thing is powerfully clear throughout Daniel chapter 6: God rules! Nations rise and nations fall, but God's plan *will* go forward according to *His* timetable. That should give us great hope as we see Daniel exactly where God had placed him. We will also see that God is unfettered by Man's pronouncements. Darius, the new leader, was a man of power and organization; he had great skill and intellect. He held no loyalty to the God of Israel, and yet as we read in the sixth chapter, we find that he had knowledge of Daniel's Jehovah.

Daniel was no longer a young man. It is likely that he was nearing ninety years of age. Through all the intervening years, he had remained faithful to God and was a committed witness. Far from being "on the shelf," his experience was utilized both by Darius and by God. We can see from his longevity in the Babylonian and then the Medo-Persian empires that Daniel was a man of wisdom, a dynamic leader, and a capable administrator.

Added to those traits was a close relationship with Jehovah, which afforded Daniel the ability to interpret dreams and visions. He was God's man for that time and in that place. The "king's heart is in the hand of the LORD . . . He turns it wherever He wishes" (Proverbs 21:1). God turned the heart of Darius toward a Hebrew man and placed that man in a strategic place of authority.

Often when Believers are set in a place of authority, it is not long before the Enemy raises his ugly head, determined to target the faithful—and Daniel was no exception. Soon others in the court were plotting:

> So the governors and satraps sought to find some charge against Daniel concerning the kingdom; but they could find no charge or fault, because he was faithful; nor was there any error or fault found in him. Then these men said, "We shall not find any charge against

this Daniel unless we find it against him concerning the law of his God." —Daniel 6:4–5

There were no charges of adultery, no Watergate break-ins, no errant emails, no Iran-Contra Affairs, no hidden bodies in the attic or the basement. The accusers could find no fault with Daniel; his life was exemplary, his record one of integrity and faithfulness. He was a target in good standing for the Fellowship of the Offended. The jealous men had to resort to subterfuge in order to trap their rival. Daniel was widely known for his custom of praying three times each day with his face pointed toward Jerusalem. The pattern had long been established, so his adversaries took advantage of Daniel's prayer routine and approached the king:

> King Darius, live forever! All the governors of the kingdom, the administrators and satraps, the counselors and advisors, have consulted together to establish a royal statute and to make a firm decree, that whoever petitions any god or man for thirty days, except you, O king, shall be cast into the den of lions. Now, O king, establish the decree and sign the writing, so that it cannot be changed, according to the law of the Medes and Persians, which does not alter. —Daniel 6:6–8

Sneaky, weren't they? As the plotters sought to spring their trap, Daniel's name was not mentioned. It would have alerted the king to the nefarious scheme of his palace officials. And, not to be overlooked, the king was flattered by all this attention. Who wouldn't want to be God for a month! Obviously, Darius wanted all the accolades and adoration, so he succumbed to the temptation and signed the decree. He was swept away on a tide of egoism and pressed his signet ring into the wax on a document that would become law, one that could not be changed. The thing was done—bow to any God except Darius and become lion fodder.

When Daniel heard of the new law that had been imposed, what do you suppose he did—wring his hands and cry, "Why me, God?" Did he begin to look for a secret place to pray or fashion a plan of escape? Did he close all the windows and lock the doors? No! Verse 10 exclaims:

> Now when Daniel knew that the writing was signed, he went home. And in his upper room, with his windows open toward Jerusalem, he knelt down on his knees three times that day, and prayed and gave thanks before his God, as was his custom since early days.
> —Daniel 6:10

Fear did not rule Daniel's life. God had been faithful to him and to his friends. Daniel had no reason to doubt. He would either be protected in the lions' den, or he would not. It made no difference; he was committed to doing the will of God. He refused to compromise his beliefs to gain the favor of the king.

The obvious happened: The men who had lain in wait for Daniel to make a misstep were overjoyed. When they saw Daniel kneeling at his window, his face toward the Holy City, they gleefully ran to the king:

> Have you not signed a decree that every man who petitions any god or man within thirty days, except you, O king, shall be cast into the den of lions? . . . That Daniel, who is one of the captives from Judah, does not show due regard for you, O king, or for the decree that you have signed, but makes his petition three times a day. —Daniel 6:12, 13

Darius likely felt as if he had been hit right in the solar plexus! He was stunned by this turn of events: A man he greatly admired was now in dire straits because of Darius's egotism.

Daniel's detractors were shouting, "That Hebrew, that foreigner, refused to obey the king! Now you must obey the decree you have signed and toss him to the lions." Let me assure you that these were not lion cubs, nor were there only one or two in the den, as we often see in illustrations. There were a sufficient number of lions to rip Daniel to shreds and devour him in but a matter of minutes.

Daniel was summarily arrested and led to the lair where the lions were incarcerated. He was cast inside and a huge stone was brought to cover the mouth of the den. King Darius then with his signet ring set his initials in the wax on the stone used to seal the entrance and returned to his palace. So distressed was the king that he spent the night silently fasting. In other words, in his sleeplessness he didn't call for the musicians, or the dancing girls, or other diversions. The Bible says, "And he could not sleep." I can believe he spent the night pacing in his bedchamber. At the earliest opportunity, he burst forth from his room and went in search of an answer:

> At the first light of dawn, the king got up and hurried to the lions' den. When he came near the den, he called to Daniel in an anguished voice, "Daniel, servant of the living God, has your God, whom you serve continually, been able to rescue you from the lions?" Daniel answered, "May the king live forever! My God sent his angel and he shut the mouths of the lions. They have not hurt me, because I was found innocent in his sight. Nor have I ever done any wrong before you, Your Majesty."
> —Daniel 6:19–22 NIV

Doesn't it seem a bit late for Darius to question whether or not Daniel was safe? It seems that every seed Daniel had sown into the king's life erupted at the mouth of the lions' den in the words, "Daniel, servant of the living God, has your God, whom you serve . . ." He wanted to know if everything Daniel had said to him was true. Could the living God deliver, perform the miraculous, save the endangered? Darius had his answer as soon as he heard the words, "My God sent his angel, and he shut the mouths of the lions."

There is no record that Daniel offered any argument to the king before he was led away to the lions' den; only after God had vindicated him and saved him from the jaws of the ferocious beasts did he offer any defense. He knew he had been innocent of anything other than obedience to Jehovah-Shammah—the Lord who was Present in the lions' den. Daniel had sought the kingdom of God and been rewarded. Daniel's consecration had won him the favor of the king, but more importantly, it won him God's continued favor.

Just as Babylon was not devoid of trials and temptations for Daniel, neither was South Korea during my service time. There were houses of ill repute on just about every corner that catered specifically to the American military. It was a daily draw for many of the men with whom I worked, even the commanding officers, but at the age of eleven I had made a vow: "God, if you will take care of me and keep me alive until I turn twenty, I'll keep myself pure from sexual sin and I'll never take your name in vain." I thought His love was conditional and that I had to do something to earn His favor. It was bad theologically but good in a practical way.

7

*For I know the plans I have for you,
declares the Lord, plans for welfare and not for evil,
to give you a future and a hope.*

—JEREMIAH 29:11 ESV

In 1966, my tour of duty in South Korea came to an end and I was sent home. I was glad to be back on US soil but sad to leave the mountain that had become a comfortable place for me, where I'd found God in a powerful way. When I arrived in the United States, I was assigned to work at a recruitment office on Broad Street in downtown Philadelphia.

The assignment offered more freedom than the duty in Korea, but it also meant I needed to find my own place to stay. I planned to rent a room at the YMCA while I located an apartment and, with my belongings packed in the car, found my way to the local Y.

A parking garage was located across the street from the YMCA so I parked the car there and paid the attendant ten dollars extra to keep an eye on it. For the sake of security, or so I thought, I locked my wallet in the glove compartment.

The receptionist at the YMCA checked his records and told me a room was available. I asked him to hold it for me and ran back to the car to retrieve my wallet. When I arrived at the garage, the parking attendant was gone. A quick check of my parking space showed that my car was gone, too, along with everything and every dime I owned—except for the twenty-six cents in change I had in my pocket.

Alone and all but penniless, my only option was to stay at a nearby Salvation Army shelter. I was angry with myself for leaving my wallet in the car and for being duped by the parking attendant. And, frankly, I was angry with the attendant for taking everything I owned. I felt sorry for myself for having to spend a few nights with *those* people, as I thought of them. Then I realized—I was homeless, too.

Sleeping at the Salvation Army building was an eye-opening experience. Every night, I was surrounded by rows and rows of men caught in adversity—the destitute, drug addict or alcoholic who came in for a warm bed and a safe place to sleep. Our cots were in close proximity to each other, so I struck up conversations with those around me. As I talked with them, I learned that many were former soldiers who, like my father and other servicemen I'd known who served during World War II, suffered from what was then called "shell shock." It is now known as PTSD or post-traumatic stress disorder. Unlike my father, though, these men could no longer fit into the society they'd given their rationality to defend.

After a few nights at the Salvation Army, I received my army pay and was able to rent a room at the YMCA. I had arrived back in the

States with a car and a carload of possessions, but when I moved to the Y, I had only the uniforms that had been reissued by the supply sergeant, a new Bible, and a few books I had been able to gather.

As was the usual practice, the recruitment office was closed Thanksgiving weekend. I combined the holiday break with a few extra days off and spent the week alone in my sparsely furnished room. Shut off from the world in what amounted to not much more than a closet, I used the time to pray and search the Scriptures, much as I had done while on the mountain in Korea. For added discipline, I committed myself to fasting and subsisted on nothing but water those seven days. All of my time was devoted to prayer and Bible study. I needed to know what to do next—after my enlistment ended—and I needed to hear that direction from God, not from my own desires. I determined to fast, pray, and read through the New Testament until I had heard that word from God.

Pastor and author Mark Batterson penned my own thoughts precisely in his book *The Circle Maker*:

> Desperate times call for desperate measures, and there is no more desperate act than praying hard. There comes a moment when you need to throw caution to the wind and draw a circle in the sand. There comes a moment when you need to defy protocol, drop to your knees, and pray for the impossible. There comes a moment when you need to muster every ounce of faith

> you have and call down rain from heaven. . . . How desperate are you for a miracle? Desperate enough to pray through the night? How many times are you willing to circle the promise? Until the day you die? How long and loud will you knock on the door of opportunity? . . . if you learn how to pray hard . . . God will honor your bold prayers because your bold prayers honor God.

After two or three days on my knees, when it seemed that the heavens were brass and God remained silent, I pointed to a battered chair in the corner and said aloud, "Jesus, this is Your chair. If You want to come and talk with me like You did when I was eleven, I am ready to listen and obey. I want to hear Your voice again."

The response to my petitions was absolute silence; it was then that I picked up the Bible and turned to the Psalms. I intended to read the entire book, but Psalm chapter one found a place in my spirit so I read it over and over, letting the words sink deeply into my mind, soul, and spirit:

> Blessed is the one who does not walk in step with the wicked or stand in the way that sinners take or sit in the company of mockers, but whose delight is in the law of the LORD, and who meditates on his law day and night. That person is like a tree planted by streams of water, which yields its fruit in season and whose leaf does not wither—whatever they do prospers. —Psalm 1:1–3 NIV

As I read those timeless verses, I could all but hear the Lord promising me that I would be a blessed man if I meditated on His Word, did not walk in the counsel of the ungodly, did not stand in the way of sinners, or sit in the seat of the scornful. He promised I would be like a tree planted by the rivers of water, bringing forth my fruit in good season. My leaves would not wither and whatever I did would prosper. I committed that entire chapter to memory.

My spirit was encouraged but I still had time to spend alone with God, and I did not feel released to do much of anything else. I had picked up a copy of *The Cross and the Switchblade*, a book by David Wilkerson. It is the story of how he ministered to drug addicts on the streets of New York City. Moved by what I read, I came to the conclusion that perhaps God was leading me to do something similar in Philadelphia.

On Christmas Day, I attended a worship service at a church not far from where I was living. While there, a man asked me if I could give him twenty dollars. Having been recently homeless, I understood his need and gave him the money. That act of compassion left me with a mere three dollars and fifty cents.

A little after noon I arrived at a diner and went inside to eat. Reviewing the menu and specials listed on the board over the counter, I realized that I couldn't afford lunch so ordered breakfast instead—bacon, eggs, and coffee. While I waited for my food, I leafed through the pages of my Bible, and my eyes fell on a verse in 1 Corinthians.

> "What no eye has seen, what no ear has heard, and what no human mind has conceived"—the things God has prepared for those who love him—these are the things God has revealed to us by his Spirit. —1 Corinthians 2:9–10 NIV

That was encouraging. My time in the army was almost at an end, and I certainly didn't want to reenlist for a second tour. I needed to know specifically, and in a practical way, what to do.

As I thought about what I'd read I sensed the words of the Lord stirring my spirit, encouraging me to ask Him one more time what direction my life should take. So I asked, "Lord, where should I go from here?"

While seated in a booth in the corner with my Bible open before me, I felt the presence of God envelop me. As I sat there, not saying a word, only enjoying His presence, I began to think again about full-time ministry. It wasn't the first time I'd thought of that topic, but right then, with the Lord's presence close, I sensed the Holy Spirit bearing witness with my spirit that this was the direction my life should take.

After struggling with that revelation for a while, I finally bowed my head and prayed: "Lord, I don't know what I'm supposed to do, but I know You are calling me. I might be the moron, the trash my father says I am, but if you can use garbage, my life is yours."

In order to serve God effectively, I knew I needed two things:

proper training and a license as a minister of the gospel. I knew that if God called me He could, and would, empower me to accomplish His will. In order to find my place in the existing church structure, I knew I needed to be taught and ordained. It all began with training, which meant returning to school, and not just any school; it had to be a Bible school that would accept my GED and would also prepare me to serve and work as a minister of the gospel—a preacher.

I'd already talked to a friend, Bob Bartlett, about ministry and ordination. He told me, "In my opinion, there are two good schools in our denomination—Northwestern in Minnesota, and Southwestern in Texas."

Through the window next to my table in the diner I could see the sidewalks outside covered in snow. Plows had cleared the street and the snow was piled on either side. It was bitterly cold, too, but for what was surely a God-given revelation in that moment, I thought of Texas. As I did, images from my time at Fort Sam Houston played through my mind. No doubt about it, the weather down there in Texas was quite different from what we experience in the Northeast. My heart quickened at the thought of returning to the South and a smile spread across face. God had a definite plan for my life, and it seemed it would take me through Texas.

Is it that easy? I wondered as I stared out the window. *Is that what You're saying to me? Do you want me to go to Texas?* The idea of doing that seemed right to my spirit and I asked the Lord, "Is that what you want me to do? Go to Texas and attend Bible school?" Right there, as

I was seated in that booth, eating breakfast for my Christmas lunch, I sensed Him saying, "Go."

A few weeks after Christmas, I located the address for Southwestern Assemblies of God College in Waxahachie, Texas, and wrote for a course catalog and application. When it arrived in the mail, I flipped through the catalog pages and knew immediately that this school was the place for me. I applied and was accepted for the fall term. It was another answer to prayer. During the years that followed, God would answer yet another prayer—that of finding a godly woman to share my life and ministry.

It was obvious to me that God was leading in ways I had not imagined. While reading through the New Testament in my room at the YMCA, I had rediscovered 1 Corinthians 2:9:

> But as it is written, Eye hath not seen, nor ear heard, neither have entered into the heart of man, the things which God hath prepared for them that love him. (KJV)

The Old Testament prophet Elijah trusted God completely and depended on Him for survival, and because of the prophet's biblical example, I had no hesitation in following God's lead to a small town in central Texas just south of the growing metropolis of Dallas.

Like Elijah who obeyed God whether in the glare of the spotlight or hidden in a cave by a stream; whether eating the finest cut of meat or food delivered daily by birds, I wanted to follow God faithfully. Elijah placed his very life in God's hands, submitting to Jehovah's commands immediately and without question or hesitation. When the drought worsened and the brook dried up, God dispatched the prophet on a long, arduous, and dangerous walk from the cave by the brook Cherith all the way to the Mediterranean coast. His destination was Zarephath; his next hiding place was the home of a widow and her only son. God had instructed Elijah to ask the widow for bread and water. Her answer must have stunned the prophet:

> As surely as the LORD your God lives," she replied, "I don't have any bread—only a handful of flour in a jar and a little olive oil in a jug. I am gathering a few sticks to take home and make a meal for myself and my son, that we may eat it—and die. —1 Kings 17:12 NIV

Jehovah breathed the solution into Elijah's spirit, and he replied:

> Don't be afraid. Go home and do as you have said. But first make a small loaf of bread for me from what you have and bring it to me, and then make something for yourself and your son. —1 Kings 17:13 NIV

That instruction must have been humbling—the great prophet of God sent to eat a piece of flatbread from the last smidgen of flour and oil the widow possessed. And Elijah was not to give; he was to take. As a prophet of God accustomed to the miraculous, he surely must have wanted to be the one to provide an abundant supply for this widow—a room filled with oil, flour, lentils, vegetables—but no.

Like the children of Israel who received manna sufficient for the day (see Exodus 16:4), God supplied a daily quantity of flour and oil for the widow, her son, and her houseguest. She had trusted God for provision; Jehovah-Jireh—the God who Provides—answered.

Because the widow offered Elijah the last of her food, God miraculously supplied her needs:

> The bin of flour was not used up, nor did the jar of oil run dry, according to the word of the LORD which He spoke by Elijah. —1 Kings 17:16

I was equally determined to follow God's direction as I set out for Waxahachie, Texas, college, and whatever exploits God had planned for my life.

8

*He who finds a wife finds a good thing
and obtains favor from the Lord.*

—Proverbs 18:22 esv

Not long after I arrived on campus I became acquainted with a young woman whose name was Linda. After talking with her on several occasions I asked her out on a date. In that time and place, a date consisted of attending a church service and then going out to eat with friends. It wasn't that big a deal, but with the emotional scars I still carried from my childhood, the most difficult part wasn't the date itself; it was finding the courage to ask her. Still, Southwestern was a Christian college and I assumed she would at least respond in a kind and gracious manner.

Much to my surprise, instead of a gracious response she struck an arrogant pose with her hands on her hips and replied haughtily, "I'll never date you. I intend to marry someone who will make something of himself."

I wasn't asking her for a commitment, just to join me for church and a burger afterward, but I understood why she wasn't interested. I didn't come from a background of money or privilege. The money I did have was earned by working as a maintenance man on campus—a mere thirty-two cents per hour. I didn't have nice clothes to wear—they'd been stolen when my car went missing in Philadelphia, and my father wasn't a pastor. I wasn't conversant with the popular buzzwords of the day. In short, I wasn't "cool."

Her unabashed rejection of me—along with the scathing assessment of my potential future, or lack thereof—reopened emotional wounds in a way that I hadn't expected to encounter at a Christian college. Recovering from that took a while. Not because I was particularly attached to her, but because I had not expected to be skewered in the process.

Over the next several months, I backed away from the notion of *dating* and allowed my association with women on campus to evolve more naturally, and without a hint of romance. As a consequence, I developed a number of casual friendships. One of those friendships was with a young woman whose given name, Carolyn, means "joy." Carolyn Wedel was a fellow student who attended several of the same classes with me. We studied together and she sought my advice when dating others.

Sometime during those first few months in school, a group of us signed up to conduct worship services for a congregation a few miles outside Waxahachie. Carolyn was part of that group. It was raining when we arrived and I held an umbrella over her as we made our way to the door of the church.

As the year progressed, Carolyn and I spent more and more time together, even though she dated other men. Sometimes we studied together in the library, other times we rode up to South Dallas for worship at Oak Cliff Assembly of God Church. With Carolyn in the car, the drive to Dallas didn't seem all that far. In fact, it was much too short and time passed far too quickly.

After the Sunday-night services, we sometimes rode over to Kip's Big Boy, a restaurant not far from the church, where we had dinner or dessert. Often we went with a group, but even when it was just the two of us there was nothing consciously romantic about those times we were together. I didn't attempt to kiss her or insist that she sit close beside me in the car. I just concentrated on being the best gentleman I could be and enjoying her company. She told me she felt the same way. We liked spending time together—which I suppose was the most romantic pursuit a couple can have.

Carolyn continued to date others, but when each of those relationships ended, I was the one she turned to for comfort. When other boys wanted to date her, she would come to me and ask my advice. Guys who were interested in her also came to me for advice.

One fellow named Doug was particularly interested in her and asked me everything—her favorite flower, food, and a dozen other things. I knew all of those things about her because I'd paid attention when she talked. One day, after they'd been dating for a while, Doug even asked me if I thought he should kiss her. That was the one question I couldn't answer. Deep inside I didn't want to answer it. Did he really have to ask me about that? And if he did, maybe that said more about where things were with them than he realized.

"They're *her* lips," I finally quipped. "You'll have to ask her."

Carolyn and I never really had a "first date." We were together as friends many times; we just never thought of it as "dating." I don't think I wanted to think of it that way, either. Over the course of that first year, she had become the most important person in my life. I was afraid that if I tried to take things in an overtly romantic direction, she might not be interested and that would make it all but impossible for us to continue being friends. If it was friendship or nothing with her, I wanted all the friendship I could get. In the secret place that no one reveals to anyone, however, I knew that I was in love with her and had been since almost the first time I saw her smile.

One Sunday, she and I rode up to her home church in Fort Worth and joined her parents, Neil and Peggy, for the morning worship service. Afterward, we went over to their home for lunch. As we walked through the back door I heard music playing in the background. The aroma of a roast cooking in the oven filled the air. It was the most peaceful home I'd ever entered.

I thought, *This is what I'm looking for. This right here. This kind of family. This kind of home. I want a family just like this.*

That summer, Carolyn traveled to Jamaica on a missions trip. While she was gone, I realized that not only did I love her, I wanted to marry her. That was a big step for me and although I was sure she felt something similar for me, I remained guarded in expressing my feelings for her. I wrote her throughout the summer, but they were newsy missives. More like a report of what I'd done and what was happening than the longing of a lover for his beloved. Meanwhile, her roommate on the trip received romantic letters from her boyfriend. Carolyn was not impressed by my letters, and I think she began to wonder just what sort of fellow I really was.

When she returned from Jamaica, I blurted out the question that had been on my heart and mind during her absence, "Will you marry me?" She wasn't very enthusiastic at first and, in fact, told me she would have to pray about it. In retrospect, I think she might have given me that response even if she'd been wildly enthusiastic. By then she knew enough about me to know that I had endured a lot of pain in my life; I'm sure she wondered how much unresolved emotional baggage I still carried with me. I didn't blame her, as I often wondered the same thing. I was determined to not turn out like my father, and I had no intention of letting Carolyn slip away, either.

It was difficult, but I gave her space and allowed her time to seek God's direction and then to make up her own mind. We continued to see each other, just as before, and I did my best to do everything possible to show her how much I cared for her. But I avoided the question of marriage for a while and was determined not to press for an answer.

Eventually Carolyn accepted my proposal and we set the wedding date for November 29, 1969—the Saturday following Thanksgiving. While neither of my parents attended the ceremony, my sisters, Bonnie and Sheila, did. I was glad to have them share that moment with me. Aunt Ginger, my mother's sister, was unable to attend, but she sent us a gift of two hundred dollars. It was all the money we had at that time and seemed like a small fortune. We used it to furnish our apartment after the wedding.

I loved this beautiful blonde more than life itself, and that devotion has only increased through the years she has been by my side. Carolyn was the first person ever to believe in me and I entrusted my heart to her—except for one little corner. It was perhaps the most important corner of all—my childhood of abuse and my fear of rejection was tucked away behind that door and secured by a lock and key that defied entry. The door of that sealed room had never been opened to the woman who suddenly shared my life. At no time had I ever allowed her to see the wounded child, the driven little boy crying out for love and acceptance. After she finally met my father, she told me she was grateful that I had not told her of my abusive upbringing. Carolyn had been raised in a loving Christian home and admitted tearfully that she might not have married me had she known more of my background. She had been taught as a child to marry a person of the same faith and who was from a godly home. In no way did that describe my childhood household.

God had answered my prayer for a virtuous, loving helpmate as He had answered the prayers of many others before me. Following

God's direction in choosing a mate is crucial to the quality of your life. If you don't believe that, Ahab is a good example. His choice of Jezebel as a mate set Israel on a disastrous course. Another is Samson and Delilah, or the many wives and concubines of Solomon.

None of these men married women of faith capable of rearing godly children. Men of God, men of faith, integrity, and character will prayerfully seek divine direction in seeking a wife and helpmate.

Proverbs 31 is perhaps the benchmark description of a godly wife. Verses 10–12 provide insight:

> Who can find a virtuous and capable wife? She is more precious than rubies. Her husband can trust her, and she will greatly enrich his life. She brings him good, not harm, all the days of her life. (NLT)

Abraham's prayer for a wife for his beloved son, Isaac, is an excellent illustration of Jehovah's provision. Just as God answered my prayer for a mate, so He answered when that patriarch of old prayed for wisdom and direction. Not wanting Isaac to take a wife from among the idol worshipers in Canaan, Abraham called in his most trusted servant, Eliezer, and said:

> Swear by Jehovah, the God of heaven and earth, that you will not let my son marry one of these local girls, these Canaanites. Go instead to my homeland, to my relatives, and find a wife for him there. —Genesis 24:3–4 TLB

The servant had ten camels loaded with provisions, including gifts of gold, silver, and fine clothing for a prospective bride. He then set out toward Nahor, the home of Abraham's nephew Bethuel. How would he know God's choice for Isaac? Nearing the village, the servant paused at a well and sought the direction of Jehovah:

> "O Jehovah, the God of my master," he prayed, "show kindness to my master Abraham and help me to accomplish the purpose of my journey. See, here I am, standing beside this spring, and the girls of the village are coming out to draw water. This is my request: When I ask one of them for a drink and she says, 'Yes, certainly, and I will water your camels too!'—let her be the one you have appointed as Isaac's wife. That is how I will know." —Genesis 24:12–14 TLB

Soon, a lovely young woman, Rebekah, approached the well with her water jug. Eliezer asked her for a drink of water. She lowered the jug into the well, offered him a drink, and then filled the watering trough with as many jugs as necessary to slake the thirst of his camels. (A single camel can drink up to thirty gallons of water in just a few minutes!) Abraham's retainer presented the young woman with a golden ring and bracelets. Rebekah hurried home to tell her father, Bethuel, and her brother, Laban, what had happened. Laban raced to the well to greet the man and invite him to their home.

The family must have been stunned to hear the story of Abraham's success and of his beloved son for whom he wished to provide a bride. The family agreed that it was God's will for Rebekah to return to Canaan with Abraham's trusted manservant. She readily consented to go with Eliezer at once. The Bible doesn't tell us exactly how Jehovah may have prepared her heart to receive the proposal of marriage to Isaac, but it seems obvious from her ready response that He had.

After the long journey from her homeland to Beer Lahai Roi in the Negev where Abraham had pitched his tents, Rebekah spotted a man in the distance and asked to be let down from the camel's back.

> "Who is that man walking through the fields to meet us?" she asked the servant. And he replied, "It is my master's son!" So she covered her face with her veil.
>
> Then the servant told Isaac the whole story. And Isaac brought Rebekah into his mother's tent, and she became his wife. He loved her very much, and she was a special comfort to him after the loss of his mother.
> —Genesis 24:65–67 TLB

Abraham had encircled Isaac, Eliezer, and his future daughter-in-law with prayer; and God had miraculously provided. From the union of Isaac and Rebekah would spring forth Jacob (whose name God later changed to Israel). After centuries of both blessings and hardship, a child would be born through the lineage of Judah, a son of Jacob. He is Jesus Christ, the Savior of the world.

The efficacy of our prayers is not determined by our dexterity with whatever language we speak. It is not dependent on a prescribed repetitious prayer. God knows our hearts before we ever bow a knee and utter a word. Many have asked the question: Why pray if God is omniscient—all-knowing? Prayer is not about imparting knowledge to God; it is about having fellowship with Him. We desire to spend time in communion with our heavenly Father and to seek His will. "Not my will, but thine, be done" was Jesus' prayer in the garden of Gethsemane. Prayer is an act of surrender to the will of God, of aligning ourselves with His plan and purpose for our lives.

9

*I will instruct you and teach you in the way you should go;
I will guide you with My eye.*

—PSALM 32:8

Carolyn and I had been married about a month when a call came from Dwayne Duck, a pastor from North Little Rock, Arkansas. We had all attended Southwestern College together, and Dwayne had been called to pastor a church in the Little Rock suburb. He told me about Troy Collier, a man attempting to open a Teen Challenge center in the area. Collier was looking for a couple to direct the work at the center and asked Dwayne if he might recommend a candidate. Dwayne immediately thought of Carolyn and me and called to ask if we would be interested in the position.

Having worked for a time with Teen Challenge before leaving the army, I understood how the program operated and was intrigued by the possibility of building a center from the ground up—facility, personnel, and program. Carolyn was also familiar with the ministry from her experience growing up in an Assemblies of God congregation. Teen Challenge, a residential substance abuse and recovery program, is sanctioned and administered by that denomination. A note from the Teen Challenge website asserts:

> Certainly we cannot claim a magical cure for addiction . . . all we can say is that we have found a power that captures a person more strongly than narcotics but He captures only to liberate.

Carolyn had never been involved in the day-to-day operation of such a residential program. Still, she was interested in the possibilities it afforded and excited about the prospect of us ministering together.

Dwayne's call came near the end of our third semester at the college. We began to pray about the opportunity and weigh the pros and cons of taking the job. Leaving Texas meant that we would not have completed the courses required to graduate. It was a difficult decision because I had traveled to Texas in response to the specific leading of the Holy Spirit. Carolyn and I drew a prayer circle around Dwayne's proposition and began to earnestly intercede for God's direction. We knew that, according to Proverbs 15:29, "The LORD is far from the wicked, but he hears the prayer of the righteous" (NIV).

Over the next few weeks, we began to sense that the Holy Spirit was leading us to accept the offer from Troy and take the supervisory role. The next challenge and opportunity for prayer came when we began to try to pack our belongings into Carolyn's tiny Nash Rambler—which she'd had since high school. That trip to North Little Rock was an exercise in both faith and fortitude!

We arrived in Arkansas only to find that the ministry was exclusively a men's program. It was debt-laden and had a backlog of potential clients. Prior to our involvement, Troy and the board of directors reached an agreement with the local court to defer drug defendants to the program. When arrested, those who were willing to plead guilty were offered the option of serving out their time in our Teen Challenge program or be sentenced to incarceration in either the state's Tucker or Cummins prison. Needless to say, many chose Teen Challenge as the most appealing, and least confining, option.

Teen Challenge owned what seemed to us to be a manor in North Little Rock located a few houses down from the governor's mansion. Though it was a prestigious address, the house had not been well maintained. Shortly after we arrived, the men assigned to the program went to work cleaning and painting it. As a residential program, the guys lived at the facility. Carolyn and I lived there, too, which meant we were with them twenty-four hours a day. As newlyweds, we had no money and only one private room but were happy, content, and certain we were exactly where God wanted us to be.

Over the ensuing twelve months, we saw many young people led to faith in Christ and redeemed from a life of addictive and destructive behavior. We kept the men busy sixteen hours each day with classes, exercise, and work—anything to keep their minds off their former lifestyle and give God an opportunity to do a transformative work in them. As a result, lives were radically changed through prayer, determination, dedication, and hard work.

As the end of the year approached, we learned that Carolyn was pregnant. By then, the Teen Challenge center was established and operating with a staff that was capable of administering its programs, a board qualified to sustain the ministry, and a more than adequate facility. Long-term debt, though still an issue for the ministry, had been substantially reduced.

Sadly, Troy and I had a difference of opinion about how the ministry should operate going forward. At that point, I did the only thing I knew to do in the midst of a challenge: Carolyn and I drew a circle of prayer around that difficult situation and then we went to our knees in supplication and intercession. We were not attempting to maneuver God to our way of thinking but were simply concentrating our prayers on the need closest to our hearts. Was God about to make another change in our lives? As we began to seek God about the pending birth of our child, the work in Arkansas, and the direction our lives should take, we agreed that moving back to Texas would have the added benefit that our child would be born there. The Lone Star State was a family home for Carolyn and rapidly becoming home for me, too, but that move back to Texas was not yet to be.

Some time passed after the birth of our baby girl, Michelle, before we received an invitation to participate in a denominational ministry located in Chicago. We again went to prayer to seek God for an answer, and we felt it was His direction that we not return to Texas. We packed our belongings into the same old Rambler and tucked Michelle between us (the days before specially designed car seats).

We pointed the nose of that little car toward the north and headed for Illinois.

The work in Chicago was a rewarding experience. I spent long hours talking to people on the street, and also opened a coffee house as a gathering place for young people from the community. It was in Chicago that the Holy Spirit revealed to me what was to be the most drastic change in my ministry. I had never been able to overcome the fact that I was unable to defend my Jewish mother from my Evangelical Christian father's drunken, anti-Semitic tirades. During a two-day prayer vigil, the Holy Spirit spoke to my spirit and reminded me of how helpless I'd felt in wanting to defend my mother.

I was also reminded of the courage I had found after my transforming encounter with Him in my bedroom that long-ago night when I was a boy of eleven. Remembering all of that, I again drew a circle of prayer around what I thought was my having failed my mother. I began to seek God for deliverance from what I saw as my failure. It was then that the Lord whispered, "I AM GOING TO REDEEM ALL OF THOSE YEARS. YOU COULDN'T DEFEND YOUR MOTHER, BUT YOU WILL BECOME A DEFENDER OF MY PEOPLE. ISRAEL AND HER PEOPLE WILL BECOME THE MOTHER YOU WANTED TO DEFEND AS A CHILD. YOU WILL DEFEND THEM NOW."

The voice of the Holy Spirit was as clear in my spirit as if He had spoken to me aloud. I knew He was calling me to something fresh and new—a task that not only resonated in my spirit but energized my heart and my mind. "Okay, Lord," I said. "I will do whatever you tell me to do." I had no idea at that moment that God would call us to leave Chicago and once again return to Texas, the state that would ultimately become our base of operations. We desired more than anything to be obedient to the will of God.

When you hear the word *obedience* in the biblical context of going where God directs, do you think immediately of Abram (later named Abraham) who obeyed God's instruction to leave his homeland and set out for an unknown destination? Abram, according to tradition, worked for his idol-building father, Terah. As a young man, however, Abram began to doubt the value of worshiping gods made of precious metals, wood, and stone. He began to believe that the world had been made by one Creator. He tried to share his beliefs with his father, but to no avail. One day, in his father's absence, Abram took a hammer and smashed all his father's idols except the largest one. In the hands of that stone god, he placed the hammer used to wreak havoc on his father's stock. When he was questioned by a distraught Terah, Abram replied that the largest of the statues had destroyed the others. Terah cried: "Don't be ridiculous. These idols have no life or power. They can't do anything." Abram replied, "Then why do you worship them?"

One day as Abram was going about his usual activities, God called to him:

> Go from your country, your people and your father's household to the land I will show you. I will make you into a great nation, and I will bless you; I will make your

name great, and you will be a blessing. I will bless those who bless you, and whoever curses you I will curse; and all peoples on earth will be blessed through you.
—Genesis 12:1-3 NIV

Abram was living in Ur of the Chaldeans when God called him forth. Shortly after his very first conversation with the Creator, his father gathered the family together—Abram, Sarai, and Lot, his grandson—and started out for Canaan. When they reached Haran, however, the family settled. (Do we too often "settle" instead of actively pursuing what God has called us to do?) Sometime after his father's death, Abram gathered his family and crossed the Euphrates River, making their way down to Canaan.

I envision a contemplative Abram sitting on a bench outside the front flap of his tent. Sarai, his wife, is likely overseeing the servants as they go about their daily tasks–sweeping out the tents, beating the rugs, winnowing grain, hauling water for the animals, spinning wool, or roasting a goat or camel.

Suddenly, Abram finds himself in an encounter with Jehovah God. Perhaps God had pursued others who failed to answer His call, or who had simply answered with the most dangerous word in the Bible: tomorrow. Obviously, the Creator saw a trait in Abram that prompted Him to declare, "That's my man! He's the one with whom I'll make a covenant. He is the man for the job!" In Genesis 12:1, Abram was stunned to hear the voice of the Lord calling to him: "Get out of your country, from your family and from your father's house, to a land that I will show you."

Abram responded with great faith. He was not a young whippersnapper when the call went out; he was approximately seventy-years old. God's plan for the man who would become the father of nations didn't end when he neared the promised land; it was a plan for the Ages. Abram, later as Abraham, was to produce the lineage from which the Savior of the world would come.

Just imagine the conversation Abram must have had later that day with Sarai:

> "Wife, we're leaving first thing in the morning. God told me to go. Have the servants take down the tents, gather the flocks, pack everything, and load the camels."
>
> "Abram, what do you mean we're leaving? We can't leave. Where are we going? How long will we be gone?"
>
> "Yes, Sarai, we are leaving, and we won't be coming back to Haran. God told me that He would lead us to the promised land—the land of Canaan. I just know I have to follow His instructions."
>
> "Where is Canaan, Abram?"
>
> "I don't know, dear. God will direct us as we go; I just know we have to go."

It was a little different for Carolyn and me; we knew the decision to leave Chicago was much bigger than simply relocating. We were certain we had been called to the ministry and, following that weekend of prayer and petition, equally certain our work would somehow involve the people of Israel. In human terms we, like Abram, were striking out on our own. In spiritual terms we were off on a God-ordained adventure. Where would God lead us and how would He get us there?

In Chicago we had lived in a small apartment and didn't own much except a bed, a table and chairs, and a television set. Michelle's belongings and the things necessary to care for her comprised the majority of our possessions. We had no money and once we left the ministry where we'd been working, we had no regular income. To fund this new work, we decided to sell our furniture. I placed an advertisement in the newspaper and the first person to respond purchased it all, leaving us with one mattress and Michelle's things. Like Abram who had been called out of Ur, when God said, "Go," Carolyn and I began packing our meager belongings.

Sometime during the night before our departure, Carolyn and I both came down with stomach flu. We spent hours crawling on our hands and knees to the bathroom and praying that Michelle would be spared that debilitating bug. The next day, weak but determined, we climbed into our old, dilapidated car and made our way to a church in Columbus, Indiana, for a speaking engagement. The pastor had gone on a trip to Florida, intending to return in time for the Sunday service. While he was away, a blizzard moved through the region, making it impossible for him to return home. Only a handful of people braved the terrible conditions to attend the service that morning—not exactly the kind of beginning we'd imagined as we set off for Texas and home.

After the service, we waded through the snow and ice only to find our car reduced to a still-smoldering hulk. A short in the wiring had caused a fire, and the car was totally consumed, along with everything we owned. It was the second time in my life I had lost everything in a car-related disaster. However, what seemed a catastrophe was simply an opportunity for God to perform yet another miracle.

One of the people who attended the service at the church was a man named Gene Darnell. I learned later that he was a serious believer and genuine intercessor. He saw our predicament, loaded us into his car, and took us home with him for the night. The next morning, as we pondered how we were going to get to Texas, Gene handed me the keys to a brand-new Buick Electra. Carolyn and I were astounded and speechless. We had no idea how to respond to his generosity.

"I was praying about your situation," Gene explained. "God told me to give you the car."

To say that we were overjoyed would be an understatement, and right there in his house Gene became our first ministry partner. He, like Abraham of old, believed in things that were not seen as though they already existed (see Romans 4:17). We left that day to continue on our way, amazed and overwhelmed at the way God had provided. It was but a foretaste of what God could and would do in our lives and ministry.

10

And my God shall supply all your need according to His riches in glory by Christ Jesus.

—PHILIPPIANS 4:19

Carolyn and I walked around that new vehicle in wonder, praise, and thanksgiving for God's provision. What a blessing! What an answer to prayer! We were ecstatic and so grateful for God's miraculous intervention in our lives. With only the barest of necessities, we climbed inside that beautiful car and once again headed toward home.

On our way back to Texas we drove through Arkansas. When we reached Little Rock, a sign in the distance that advertised a mobile-home sales lot captured our attention. We decided to stop, stretch our legs, and "window shop" for a few minutes. That was our idea; God had another plan that day. Carolyn and I had surrounded our need for a place to live. A small mobile home was certainly an option. It would provide a place to eat and sleep and a roof over our heads, although we had no idea how we might pay for the privilege of that shelter.

As we walked the lot, stopping to admire the various models, we were clueless that God was hard at work on our behalf.

Inside the business office was the owner, Bill Roetzell. He made time in his schedule for daily devotions—a time he spent in prayer and Bible study. When we arrived he was on his knees, seeking God for direction for his day's activities. When he finished communing with God he stood and looked out the window. As he did, he saw us on the lot. In that moment the Holy Spirit spoke to him, "You are to give them a new mobile home," the Lord said, "but not from the lot. It must come from the factory."

A few minutes later, Bill walked out onto the property and told us what he'd heard. We were speechless. "There's only one thing," he added.

"What's that?"

"You'll need something to tow it with."

"Like what?"

"Well, it'll take a car at least the size of a . . ." He paused while he thought, then said, "At least the size of a Buick Electra."

I laughed. "That's exactly what we have."

"Then you're all set. I'll have a trailer hitch put on it for you."

Carolyn and I stared at each other, totally speechless. Again, God had seen the need that we had surrounded with prayer and entered that circle to meet our necessity. We left Little Rock in awe of God's provision. The home Bill had given us would also become our ministry headquarters. When it arrived, we set it up in the Santa Dee Trailer Court in Fort Worth, and I carved out a small corner for my office. When people asked, I referred to it as "Our international headquarters for ministry to the nation of Israel." Many laughed and some retorted, "You've got delusions of grandeur." What they failed to realize was that the God of the universe, the Creator of all, had honored our circle of prayer. He was—and is—ready and eager to meet the needs of His children and had answered our plea for a place to call home.

Our little house on wheels was thirty-two feet long and eight feet wide with a six-feet-high ceiling—several inches below my six-feet-five-inch head. In my frequent rushes to get from the front to the back, my head too often smashed the lightbulbs that got in my way. In order to shower, I was forced to kneel in the tub as if in an attitude of prayer. Yes, it was small and confining, but God had blessed us first of all with a place to keep our baby girl safe, and secondly with our second ministry partner, Bill Roetzell.

After a year of living in our claustrophobic quarters and with a toddler literally under our feet, Carolyn and I began to beseech God to provide a larger place with higher ceilings so I wouldn't have to fear walking down the hall. Isaiah has long been one of my favorite books of the Bible, so what the prophet had written in chapter fifty-four, verse two seemed fitting:

> Make your tent larger, stretch your tent curtains farther out! Spare no effort, lengthen your ropes, and pound your stakes deep. (NET)

Carolyn and I had yet another need to surround with prayer: We were seeking God's will and direction for a larger home to house our family and our ministry. Sadly, our coffers were empty; we had nothing to invest. It seemed humanly impossible that we could find anything we might be able to afford. We were, however, encouraged by the Holy Spirit that our request was in order with God's desire to provide a place of shelter.

After weeks of kneeling inside our prayer circle with God, thoroughly engaged in prayer and supplication, we happened upon a small house on Dream Lane in Watauga, a Fort Worth suburb. To our wondering eyes, it seemed like a veritable "McMansion." At the very least, I could walk through the rooms without dashing my head against a lightbulb. I contacted the owner of the house and was told that he wanted a down payment of thirty-two hundred dollars. Fortunately for a family with no credit history, he was willing to finance the remainder of the price himself, a factor most decidedly in my favor.

Sensing that this was definitely the will of God, I made a commitment to purchase the property and informed the owner that I would return the following Monday with the down payment. As we backed out of the drive on that Friday afternoon, Carolyn reminded me that we were only thirty-two hundred dollars short of what we needed. With the confidence that only the Holy Spirit can instill, I replied calmly, "In my spirit, I am certain the money will be here by Monday." On Saturday, our mailbox was empty, but I was filled with God's assurance that He would provide.

When Carolyn and I had been in Arkansas with Teen Challenge, we had met Charles Capps, a cotton farmer, land developer, and dynamic Bible teacher. Monday morning I opened our mailbox and there was a letter from Charles. Inside was a check for exactly thirty-two hundred dollars. As soon as I got home, I called him and asked, "What is the check for?"

He exclaimed, "Don't *you* know what it's for?"

"Yes, I do," I answered, suddenly feeling rather foolish for having asked. I'd believed God, He sent the money, and then I had the nerve to act surprised!

Carolyn and I cashed the check and took that money to the owner of the house on Dream Lane. In a few days, the paperwork was completed and we had moved into the house. It felt great to have a home of our own—a place where we could live, and breathe, and move—without bumping into each other or the light fixtures.

Just as God had gloriously provided shelter for our small family, that same bequest of lodging was certainly extended to the biblical Ruth. The Creator has given us a clear picture of sanctuary in her life. This Old Testament story of the woman from Moab and her devotion to her mother-in-law, Naomi, is legendary.

Throughout the history of Israel Yahweh has used various means to discipline His people—pestilence, drought, famine, and more. During a period of extreme famine Elimelech, a man from Bethlehem (which means "house of bread"), traveled to the land of Moab with his wife, Naomi, and their two sons. Naomi's submission to her husband is evident: she was called upon to leave her home, her country, and her close relatives to follow her husband to a foreign land. Uprooting, leaving behind all you know intimately and hold dear and moving to a foreign land can incite a rampant case of culture shock: The food is different, the language incomprehensible, and the customs unfathomable. It is not an easy passage. That is where Naomi suddenly found herself and her family—outsiders in a strange land.

It is likely that they were spurned by the inhabitants of Moab, just as the Moabites would have been in Bethlehem. What was to be a short relocation morphed into a decade! For ten long years they were separated from their kinsmen. The two sons, Mahlon and Chilion, took Moabite women as their wives, and it is possible that the addition of the two daughters-in-law helped to assuage some of Naomi's loneliness.

As the years passed, neither woman bore children by her husband. For the women in the family it was more than the disappointment of not being able to conceive; it marked the end of Elimelech's line. There would be no one to continue the family name or reclaim a home back in Bethlehem. Nothing, however, could have prepared her for the sword that was about to fall upon their household. First Elimelech died; Naomi was suddenly a widow. Then in time, both sons died, leaving her with no means of support and only two daughters-in-law, Ruth and Orpah, to comfort her.

After hearing that the famine had ended, Naomi made the determination to return to Bethlehem in Judah, the land of her people.

Aaron Marten, writer for the *Herald* magazine wrote of the bond between the three women:

> They must have had a certain fondness both for Naomi and for Jehovah because of what Naomi said. Even if she did not directly witness to her daughters-in-law, certainly her actions and her character must have been apparent. As a good Jew, Naomi would have been careful to cook according to Jewish laws and customs and expect her daughters-in-law to do likewise.
>
> The closeness between Orpah, Ruth, and Naomi can be seen in the emotional pleadings of Naomi that they go back to the land of Moab. Naomi knew that the desire of Ruth and Orpah to find new husbands would be best served in Moab and she wanted them to be happy even at the expense of her own needs. The love between Ruth and Naomi was so strong that Ruth was willing to forsake her land, her beliefs, and her natural family.

Many weddings today include Ruth's timeless pledge to her beloved mother-in-law:

> Entreat me not to leave you, or to turn back from following after you; for wherever you go, I will go; and wherever you lodge, I will lodge; your people shall be my people, and your God, my God. —Ruth 1:16

After embarking for her homeland, Naomi halted on the way and offered emancipation to the two young women she had come to love. She encouraged them to go home to their parents, find husbands, and make new lives for themselves. To follow her meant the certainty of no shelter or place to call home, along with hardship and isolation. Like Joshua before them, they too would have to make life-altering decisions. Having come to know Yahweh under the roof of Elimelech, they were challenged to "choose for yourselves this day whom you will serve" (Joshua 24:15).

Orpah, the sensible and pragmatic one of the two daughters-in-law, finally acquiesced to Naomi's urging after much pressure and attempts to convince. Ruth refused; and in her refusal she embraced Naomi's God and her people. She turned from the darkness of paganism to the light of the God of Israel.

Ruth then made her astounding declaration of love and devotion that we find in the book of Ruth, chapter one, to her mother-in-law. What a mind-boggling pledge! What courageous submission! With both eyes open and well aware of the bleak future before her, Ruth opts to devote her life to her mother-in-law—whatever may come. This is the kind of vow God wants us to make to Him, and not just to Him—to our spouses, to our children, to His people. It takes true tenacity and perseverance to go where God sends us, to live where He directs us, to love the people He asks us to love—unconditionally. Ruth made that kind of commitment to Naomi even though the journey ahead would be long, hazardous, and stressful.

Just as God had provided for Ruth and Naomi, so had He provided me with a beautiful wife, a loving family, and a safe shelter for us. Through the years, He has continued to fulfill His Word: "And my God will supply every need of yours according to his riches in glory in Christ Jesus" (Philippians 4:19 ESV).

In the months that followed our move to Dream Lane, I contacted pastors and former classmates from Southwestern and arranged speaking engagements at any venue that would have me. God provided opportunities, and most weeks I was invited to preach in at least two churches. He also provided the results and soon we had a number of people clamoring for further ministry training. I wasn't sure what my next step was to be and so I again began to pray earnestly for God's direction.

After a few weeks of intensive prayer, I received a phone call from Rick Shultz, the business manager for David Wilkerson, founder of Teen Challenge. We knew Rick from our work with Teen Challenge in Little Rock, and through our work there had become acquainted with David.

"Dave has been praying about the direction of his ministry," Rick explained. "And he wants to give you a farm that he owns in Texas. It's on Possum Kingdom Lake. You know where that is?"

"It's near the town of Graham in the North Texas Lake Country."

"Well, he wants you to have the property and he's willing to let it go for a small price."

I was interested in the property, but a little skeptical about the small-price part of Dave's offer. Over the next few days, however, Rick and I discussed the details and the price really was small. Not only that, Dave was willing to carry the financing himself. All our ministry had to do was make the monthly payments.

After the papers were signed and we had title to the property, Dave came over and dedicated the facility. During the worship service, he prayed, "Lord, this place needs cows. Please send Mike and Carolyn some cows to help feed all the young people who will come here for training."

A few months later, two stock trailers arrived on our property. They came late at night and I had no idea what they were doing there. By morning's light, I would see the results of that heartfelt prayer of dedication: A rancher had heard a tape of David's sermon and his petition. In response, the cattleman had sent us thirty head of Black Angus cattle—producers of some of the highest-quality beef available. Not only would our trainees learn a bit of cattle husbandry, they would eat well while doing so.

11

*You **are** my hiding place and my shield;
I hope in Your word.*

—PSALM 119:114

In October 1972, I held a series of meetings in Texarkana, a town located on the Texas–Arkansas border. The drive over from our home was too far to go back and forth each day, so I stayed at the Texarkana Holiday Inn. One afternoon as I came from the parking lot, I noticed an elderly lady who was headed toward the entrance to the hotel lobby. She was carrying a suitcase, and the thought came to me that I should help her. I stepped quickly to her side and reached to open the door. "May I carry your bag for you?" I asked.

"Thank you," she replied, "but there's no need. I am but a tramp for the Lord." She spoke with a heavy European accent and when she smiled her face lit up.

That's when I realized who she was. "Corrie ten Boom!" I exclaimed like a star-struck kid. "I've read your book *The Hiding Place*. I never imagined I would ever get to meet you. Certainly not here in East Texas."

She smiled and clasped my hand. "You can carry my suitcase if you'll join me for a cup of soup."

"I would be honored," I replied.

After Corrie had checked in at the front desk, we walked to the hotel restaurant. As we enjoyed our soup, she shared with me her great love for the Jewish people.

The Ten Booms had lived in the Netherlands, where her father owned a clock shop. Their home was an apartment above the shop. In 1844, long before Corrie was born, her grandfather began a weekly prayer meeting for the peace of Jerusalem and for the Jewish people. Her father continued that tradition, even after German troops invaded the Netherlands during World War II.

Faced with Nazi atrocities, the ten Booms began rescuing their Jewish neighbors, secreting them away to a hiding place inside their home and to locations throughout the country. When the Nazis learned of the prayer meeting and of the ten Boom family's work in rescuing Jews, Corrie, her father, Casper, and sister, Betsie, were arrested and taken to the local police station. Corrie and Betsie were later sent to Ravensbrück, a notorious concentration camp; Casper died shortly after his arrest and while still in police custody.

When Corrie paused to take a spoonful of soup, I asked, "Who is your favorite Bible character?"

"David," she quickly replied. "And my favorite of his psalms is the ninety-first. God gave me that psalm on my birthday, while I was in Ravensbrück."

"Really."

"It was April fifteenth, and I said, 'Lord, today is my birthday. Could You possibly give me a birthday present?' He whispered, 'YOUR PRESENT IS PSALM NINETY-ONE.'" Then she quoted the first verse from the King James Bible: "'He that dwelleth in the secret place of the most High shall abide under the shadow of the Almighty.' Living in that shelter—*that hiding place*—means living before an audience of one and seeking Christ's affirmation above that of the world."

Corrie and I talked for a while longer, and then I carried her suitcase up to her room and said good-bye at the door. As I turned to walk away, she called to me, "Mike, you must remember what Jesus said in Jeremiah 29:13."

"What's that, Miss ten Boom?"

"You shall find me when you seek me with all of your heart."

I didn't know it then but that chance meeting with Miss ten Boom would launch a lifelong association with her story and her work.

✦ ✦ ✦

That fall I held more than forty church services and conventions. One day while in prayer, the Holy Spirit asked me, "ARE THE CHURCHES YOUR SOURCE OF INCOME, OR AM I?"

I answered, "You are!"

Challenged by Him, I canceled the remaining scheduled services and fasted and prayed for sixty days. While reading in the Gospel of Matthew, a scripture jumped from the page:

> "Assuredly, I say to you, if you have faith and do not doubt, you will not only do what was done to the fig tree, but also if you say to this mountain, 'Be removed and be cast into the sea,' it will be done." —Matthew 21:21

While praying, I sensed God calling me to end our ministry in Texas and move to another state. My best estimates indicated that making that move would cost a million dollars. As I continued to pray, I asked the Lord about that. He replied, "IT WILL BE DONE." I circled that scripture and believed with my whole heart that God would provide. I knew that if I followed God's will for me and kept my heart pure, I could indeed ask according to the things He shared through my spirit and through His Word.

At the time, we had no money to make a move and barely enough income to meet the necessities or our daily life. Michelle, our five-year-old daughter, heard us talking and said, "Daddy, I've got a million dollars." She left the room and returned with her piggy bank and handed it to me. "See, Daddy, I will give you the money. It's here in my piggy bank."

With tears in my eyes, we opened her piggy bank and counted the money. She had three dollars and twenty-six cents. I took her in my arms and wept at the kindness in her heart. As I cried out in thankfulness for her childlike faith, my own faith inreased.

As an act of obedience to God and an object lesson for Michelle, I took her offering to a bank in Graham, Texas, where we lived then, and told the banker I wanted to open an account. While he prepared the paperwork for the account, I explained that I would be depositing a million dollars there and wanted to know how I could structure the deposit to attain maximum coverage under the then FDIC insurance limits. He explained that I could not protect the entire amount but suggested a few ways to get the most the system had to offer.

"When do you expect to make this deposit?" the bank manager asked.

"I'm not sure. I don't actually have the money yet, but God has told me that I will," I replied confidently.

"And that's your plan?" he asked, rolling his eyes and trying to suppress a laugh. "You expect to just pray and a million dollars will arrive in your mailbox?"

I was more than a little put off by his response. "Yes, I intend to pray and God intends to respond."

He laughed and shook his head. "You need serious psychiatric help."

Every day, I went to the retreat center and shut myself in the prayer room with God. I formed a prayer circle around Michelle's empty piggy bank and petitioned God for help. Gradually checks began to arrive. Dr. Pat Robertson heard about our effort and sent us a check for $10,000. Pat Boone, upon hearing about our ministry plans, also contributed. Slowly people nationwide opened their wallets and funded the project.

Sixteen weeks after my initial meeting with the banker in Graham, our account at his bank held the promised million dollars. The banker shook his head in amazement and apologized for his earlier response. Michelle's offering touched the heart of God, turned His head, and moved His hand.

It took longer to coordinate the change of location than I'd hoped, but eventually we made the move. It was a change that would ultimately lead to my association with Israel's then-prime minister Menachem Begin.

12

*Call unto me, and I will answer thee,
and show thee great and mighty things,
which thou knowest not.*

—JEREMIAH 33:3 KJV

One morning, after having been battered by the Enemy into thinking God had withdrawn His hand from my ministry, and with my mood lower than low, I walked out the back door of our home, sat down on the top step, and dropped my head in my hands. As I sat there with my head bowed, I prayed, "God, my life is in Your hands. Once again, I surrender to You. Remember, You told me You loved me and had a plan for my life. Please, Lord, show me that plan."

Sitting there, spiritually prostrate before God, I heard only the rustle of the breeze as it blew through the treetops. There was no audible voice, no reminder of scripture. Nothing! I arose with no more clarification than I had when I sat down. It was then that I made a conscious decision to spiritually draw a circle around the situation, the dilemma in my life and ministry, with concentrated prayer.

The following day, I was scheduled to preach at a friend's church. Despite the encroaching depression, I had booked a few events just to keep going. As a pastor/friend was fond of saying, "Keep doing the last thing God told you to do until He tells you to do something else." So off I went, while deep inside all I really wanted was a renewed sense of calling. I wanted things to be right—between God and me—and I wanted to be at peace with myself. At that moment, I couldn't see any of that ever coming to pass. Instead, things seemed to be reaching an end. The Enemy lied that maybe God was through with me, that nothing more would come of the things of which I'd dreamed and wanted so much to accomplish.

I felt as Joshua must have when God ordered him to have the children of Israel march around Jericho for seven days. Could the leader of the Israelites secretly have wondered if it was an exercise in futility? Jehovah had given the people specific instructions regarding the city that now stood between the sojourners and their promised land, and the plan must have seemed fraught with pitfalls. The people would be exposed to possible attack from those inside the city's walls. They would be mocked and ridiculed; what good would that do? Marching around in a circle?! They were also to carry their trumpets, yet not utter a sound:

> So it was, when Joshua had spoken to the people, that the seven priests bearing the seven trumpets of rams' horns before the LORD advanced and blew the

> trumpets, and the ark of the covenant of the LORD followed them. The armed men went before the priests who blew the trumpets, and the rear guard came after the ark, while the priests continued blowing the trumpets. Now Joshua had commanded the people, saying, "You shall not shout or make any noise with your voice, nor shall a word proceed out of your mouth, until the day I say to you, 'Shout!' Then you shall shout."
> —Joshua 6:8–10

After six days of what surely must have felt like utter nonsense, they were to follow the same routine—but with two notable exceptions: They were to march seven times, and then the people were to shout in praise to Jehovah for delivering the city into their hands (verse 16). Obedience was the key to moving the hand of God.

I knew in my spirit that it was God's will for us to move to another state, but where? Even though I battled the depression of not knowing what the future held, I later made preparations to board the plane that would carry me to my next speaking engagement. As it lifted off the ground, I turned my face to the window and again sought God in prayer: *Lord, I have no joy and no peace. I'm at the end. When I finish the sermon tomorrow, that's it. I don't know what else to do but give up, once and for all. I've failed you, and I've failed myself. I'm done.* Tears rolled down my cheeks, and the sense of loneliness overwhelmed me.

It was as if I were saying good-bye to something or someone I loved very much.

In the midst of my meditations, a passage of scripture, again from the book of Isaiah, came to mind. I couldn't remember all the words, just bits and pieces of what I thought the passage said, but as I thought about it, I heard that still, small voice whisper, "CIRCLE YOUR LIFE WITH PRAYER." It was encouraging to think God might be speaking to me through His Word. Would I see His miraculous intervention in my life yet again?

My Bible was tucked inside a satchel that lay beneath the seat in front of me. I reached down, retrieved it, quickly turned to Isaiah 43, and began to read the chapter. Suddenly, there it was—verses 18–19, "Do not remember the former things, nor consider the things of old. Behold, I will do a new thing, now it shall spring forth; shall you not know it? I will even make a road in the wilderness and rivers in the desert."

I began to pray those words over and over. It seemed the prophet's words were specifically directed to me. The Holy Spirit began to whisper to me: "THIS IS NOT THE END. IT'S NOT OVER. THIS IS ONLY THE BEGINNING. I'M DOING A NEW THING IN YOUR LIFE. YOU'RE GOING BACK TO THE ORIGINAL CALLING I'VE ALREADY SHOWN YOU. YOU WILL BE A PROTECTOR OF AND ADVOCATE FOR THE NATION OF ISRAEL AND OF HER PEOPLE."

I gasped in amazement as my heart leapt with wonder. Just moments before, I'd been convinced that God had turned away from me. I had been certain that my ministry was done, and yet in an instant, I felt reaffirmed as His child. Expectation rose up in me, and my spirit was energized with a renewed sense of purpose. God was at work, accomplishing His will in me, and for me, and through me. I would become a staunch defender of Israel and her people in a way I'd never been able to do to protect my mother as a child!

Although God had spoken to me and my spirit was renewed, I still had no idea what I was to do next, but I knew God had a plan. For the remainder of that day, I sought the Lord. Slowly He impressed upon my spirit that I should travel to Israel and request a meeting with Menachem Begin, Israel's then-prime minister. Now, I'll admit that to the human mind alone, that sounds rather farfetched—go to Israel, ask for a meeting with the prime minister—but after imploring God to speak to me, and then finally hearing His voice, I wasn't about to turn my back on His direction. I was committed to following Him.

As planned, I preached at the upcoming Sunday morning service and then returned home. However, instead of going home to Carolyn to announce my retirement from the ministry, I stunned her with the announcement: "I'm going to Israel!"

She had a puzzled look. "You're going to do what?"

"I'm going to Israel to meet with Prime Minister Begin."

"How do you know this? How do you know he will even meet with you?"

"God told me to go," I replied confidently. "And He told me to ask for a meeting with Prime Minister Begin. I've run from a lot of things in my life. I can't run *from* God. I need to run . . . I want to run *to* Him."

After we talked awhile longer, she realized my mind was made up. The decision had been made. I was going to do this. I was going to follow God's leading no matter what!

The following day, I made a reservation for a flight to Tel Aviv, made a hotel reservation, and then located a fax number for the prime minister's office. With those arrangements in place, I composed a letter requesting an appointment, advising the prime minister of my planned arrival date and giving him the name of the hotel where I would be staying. When the letter was finished, I signed it, inserted it in the fax machine, and sent it off with a prayer that God would have His way. I knew that decisions like my request sent to Begin's office might take days, if not weeks, to resolve. In addition to the usual delays, Menachem Begin didn't know me and there was no compelling reason for him to meet with me. After all, I was an unknown Christian minister, not someone like Billy Graham or a noted public official. I was just a boy from the other side of the tracks, determined to obey God and watch Him order events according to His purposes.

By the end of the week no response had arrived. Still, I was undeterred in my resolve to obey the Lord, so I placed my luggage in the car, and Carolyn drove me to the Dallas/Fort Worth airport for a flight to New York, the first leg of my trip to Israel.

Several hours later, I arrived in New York City, took a room at the Plaza Hotel, and retired there to pray and read my Bible. As I did, God reminded me of another scripture from Isaiah that He had given me, this one from a time when I was on the mountain in Korea: "But those who wait on the LORD shall renew their strength; they shall mount up with wings like eagles, they shall run and not be weary, they shall walk and not faint" (Isaiah 40:31). That evening, as I sat alone in the room, I sensed the voice of God assuring me I was following His will. Furthermore, that all things would turn out right, and my strength *would* be renewed. I could feel that happening right there in the hotel room!

The following day, I departed, and after a long and tiring flight landed in Tel Aviv. I then had to engage a taxi to take me to my lodgings in Jerusalem. After checking in I asked at the desk about messages that might have been left for me, hopeful that the prime minister's office had called while I still was in flight. The hotel clerk informed me there were none. I felt a twinge of discouragement but pushed it aside and took the elevator up to my room.

For the next several days, I prayed and fasted there at the hotel, believing God was at work and that I was in the right place at the right time. Finally, one morning early in my second week, the phone on the nightstand rang. When I answered the call a voice on the other end asked, "Mike Evans?" My heart stood still. "Y-y-yes," I stammered, and the man continued. "This is Yehiel Kadashai, Prime Minister Begin's personal secretary. The prime minister has agreed to meet with you. Are you available to meet this afternoon?"

Again, it was all I could do to summon a response. "What time should I come?"

Mr. Kadashai confirmed a time and I hung up the phone. Suddenly my knees turned to jelly as I sank onto the edge of the bed, and then slid to my knees. God had honored His promise to me. I was going to meet the prime minister of Israel!

Following what was for me a milestone meeting, the Holy Spirit impressed on me that I was to be a bridge-builder between Evangelicals and the Jewish people in Israel. Missionary, writer, and theological teacher Norman Grubb wrote in his book *Rees Howells Intercessor* about the commitment to help Jewish children during World War II:

> "The Holy Spirit is just like a father... Unless He in you makes the suffering your own, you can't intercede for them. You will never touch the Throne unless you send up that real cry; words don't count at all."
>
> As usual when he [Howells] had a burden like that, he felt sure that God would have him do something. As he asked what he could do, the answer came: "Make a home for them."

Howells later wrote:

> I am willing to risk my all in order to help the Jews.... But when God speaks to you, you can never

doubt it. If what God has told you leads you into great trials, then you go back to God and turn the burden of it on Him.

God placed a burden on *my* heart unlike any other; I knew only that I had to help my people—my mother's people—in any way that He directed. This has now become my life's work. Like Howells, "I am willing to risk my all in order to help the Jews."

Shortly after God opened the door for my meeting with Prime Minister Begin in Jerusalem, I read an article in the *Jerusalem Post* about the anniversary of the death of Jonathan Netanyahu, the only casualty of what had become known in the West as the "Raid on Entebbe." The Israel Defense Forces rescued a contingent of Jews whose plane had been hijacked and flown to Entebbe, Uganda. Jonathan, the leader of that force, was the only casualty.

After being prompted by the Holy Spirit, I found an address for his father, Benzion Netanyahu, and went to his home to offer my condolences. I had no idea what might happen when I arrived, but God had paved the way for me. The elder Mr. Netanyahu was a considerate host. He greeted me graciously and invited me into his home. After he and I had visited for a few minutes, a young man walked into the room. I was then introduced to Benjamin Netanyahu, the man who would become a dear friend. He was, I guessed, about thirty years old and was dressed in a suit as if just coming from work. He carried himself with a sense of purpose.

As he glanced at me and shyly smiled, I told him of the purpose of my visit. I looked into Benjamin's eyes, and his pain at the loss of his brother was palpable. In an instant I felt the anointing of the Holy Spirit rising within me. I stood slowly, put my hand on Benjamin's shoulder, and said, "You loved your brother Jonathan as Jonathan of old loved his friend David. From the ashes of your despair will come strength from God. Yet unlike Jonathan, who died in battle defending his country, you will accede to the seat of power. One day you will become the prime minister of Israel during the most crucial time in Israel's history."

Then I asked if I could pray with him. Benjamin acquiesced, and I reached in my pocket for a small vial of oil I had purchased earlier that day at the Garden Tomb. I anointed his head with oil and prayed for God's blessings and favor upon his life.

My prayer was answered in ways neither Benjamin nor I could ever have dreamed. The following day while in a meeting with the prime minister, I asked him to appoint the elder Netanyahu's son to a government post. He did, and Benjamin's political career blossomed. At this writing, he remains prime minister of Israel. Netanyahu has been a more-than-capable leader of Israel during his tenure in office and has been compared by some to British statesman Winston Churchill.

Daily I encircle the prime minister and his government, the Jewish people, and the nation of Israel with intercessory prayer. God has, indeed, fulfilled the same promise to me that He made to

Abraham in Genesis 12:3: "I will bless those who bless you, and I will curse him who curses you."

The desire to support God's chosen people has led me to form several organizations—most notably, the Jerusalem Prayer Team, Churches United with Israel, and Friends of Zion. (A later chapter is devoted to these organizations and their outreach.)

13

For He shall give His angels charge over you,
To keep you in all your ways.

—Psalm 91:11

My desire to defend Israel and the Jewish people has frequently taken me to some dangerous places, and even more often driven me to my knees in intercessory prayer. On one occasion, the Spirit of the Lord gave me another scripture. It was Deuteronomy 31:8: "And the Lord, He is the One who goes before you. He will be with you, He will not leave you nor forsake you; do not fear nor be dismayed."

My God-ordered assignment at that time was to go into Lebanon—where civil war raged and hundreds of thousands had been killed, wounded, or displaced during the prolonged fighting. I had arranged for several containers of food and medical supplies to be distributed there.

Renting a car with a Jerusalem license plate and a prefix of 666 (common among Israeli vehicles), I set out for the border between

Israel and Lebanon with a couple of friends—Sy Rickman and the late L.W. Dollar—and a cameraman. We, either bravely or foolhardily, aimed our rental car toward Sidon, about thirty miles south of Beirut on the Mediterranean.

The cities of Tyre and Sidon are mentioned several times in the Old and New Testaments. It was to this region that God sent Elijah to Zaraphath, a Phoenician seaport on the Mediterranean Sera, to minister to a widow (see chapter 4). In the early months of His ministry, people from that area traveled to see Jesus:

> Jerusalem, Idumea, from east of the Jordan River, and even from as far north as Tyre and Sidon. The news about his miracles had spread far and wide, and vast numbers of people came to see him. —Mark 3:8 NLT

In Mark 7, we read of the Canaanite woman whose daughter was miraculously healed through her encounter with Jesus. By traveling to this region and interacting with a Gentile woman, we are subtlely reminded that the promised land deeded to Abraham stretched as far north as Sidon. It was, and is still, part of Israel's original land grant from Jehovah. My team and I were about to travel the same paths Jesus had trod.

The night before our departure was spent encompassing our trip with prayer; I had been warned by Israeli intelligence not to go into Lebanon. Sy had received word that an attack on Sidon was imminent, and advised me to cancel the trip. I told him I would indeed be going to Lebanon. To break the spirit of fear that had gripped Sy, I took one of the trash cans in the hotel room, dumped the trash on the floor, and rinsed it out. Filling it with water, I washed his feet as an act of obedience to God, and an attempt to encourage Sy and build his faith.

We left early the next morning for the border and crossed at Metula. Sy's information proved to be valid, because the city had been targeted with missiles and gunfire just minutes before our arrival. We were there in time to comfort the wounded and the grieving and to share God's love with the suffering Lebanese Muslims and Christians caught in the deadly crossfire.

From Sidon, we made our way north to Beirut. Our goal was to meet with and minister to the US troops stationed there. The trunk of my car contained medical supplies and Bibles. These were to be distributed to the troops posted on the beachhead. Upon arrival, we shared the gospel with these young men and gifted each with a Bible. I soon realized they would not be home to celebrate Christmas with their families, and asked our cameraman to record Christmas greetings from these stalwart young Marines to their families back in the States. Given the event that would soon shatter the lives of those men and women, it was, perhaps, one of the best "God ideas" ever whispered into my spirit.

Later that evening the troops returned to their barracks at Beirut International Airport, approximately five hundred yards from the beachhead. We three men unrolled our sleeping bags and made our beds on the sandy beach. A little after 6:00 a.m. the following morning

I was standing on the beachhead talking to a contingent of Marines who had just taken up their posts. Suddenly a terrific explosion rent the air. As we stood there and watched, plumes of black smoke wafted heavenward over the airport; I began to pray.

We would soon learn that as the American troops were beginning a new day, the Marine sentry at the gate looked up to see a big yellow Mercedes truck barreling down on his checkpoint. The sentry reportedly stated that the driver of the truck smiled at him as he crashed through the gates. The truck was on a course for the lobby of the barracks. The sentries, armed only with pistols, were unable to stop the speeding vehicle.

The Mercedes carried explosives equal to about six tons of TNT. The driver rammed into the lower floor of the barracks and simultaneously discharged his deadly cargo. The explosion was so great that the four-story building pancaked, each floor plummeting to the floor below, reaching the ground as a heap of rubble. Many of the dead were not killed by the blast itself, but were crushed beneath the cinder-block building.

News would soon spread that Islamic Jihad, a pseudonym for Iranian armed and funded Hezbollah terrorists, had taken credit for the attack that targeted the Marine barracks. The explosion and collapse of the building killed 241 American servicemen: 220 Marines, 18 Navy personnel, and three Army soldiers. In retaliation, the huge guns of US warships off the coast of Beirut began to shell the area.

Approximately two minutes following the blast at the Marine barracks, terrorists attacked French troops stationed at Drakkar, a building in Beirut used as a garrison. The First Parachute Chasseur Regiment lost fifty-eight paratroopers with fifteen wounded. It was the most deadly loss for the French military since the Algerian War (1954–1962). It was my introduction to how vile and deadly terror attacks can be.

My friends and I hurriedly gathered our belongings, piled in the car, and headed for Nahariya, Israel, on the border. I had followed the sea to Beirut, but it would be dark soon, and that became a problem as we drove south. I made several wrong turns that took us into Tyre and into the midst of the funeral of a Hezbollah operative. Our vehicle was an Avis Rent a Car from Jerusalem with the distinctive Israeli license plate—not a good thing to have when you're surrounded by raging, grieving terrorists. Somehow God blinded their eyes and we were able to get through the city.

Once we reached the outskirts, I made another wrong turn. Instead of going to Nahariya, we were unknowingly headed down a dirt road toward Damascus, Syria. Soon our vehicle was spotlighted and tracer bullets raced overhead, then large cannon shells began to crash into the desert around us.

We had been on God's business, and now we were being targeted! Next, our car sputtered and died. We had left Beirut so abruptly that I had forgotten to check the fuel gauge. Now we were stranded on a desert road, amid hostile fighters, and out of petrol.

What else could happen? There seemed no way to survive. It would only be a matter of minutes before our vehicle would be blown to shreds.

One of the men with me shouted, "We're dead!"

I replied, "We're not dead; you're talking! We need to pray."

Romans 8:26 offers comfort in times of trouble or potential disaster:

> Likewise the Spirit helps us in our weakness. For we do not know what to pray for as we ought, but the Spirit himself intercedes for us with groanings too deep for words. (ESV)

Charles Spurgeon said of this depth of prayer: "Groanings which cannot be uttered are often prayers which cannot be refused."

There are times when we are so burdened that we simply can't formulate words to express our agony of spirit. As patriot and founding father Thomas Paine said, "These are the times that try men's souls." We often find ourselves repeating, "Please, God," over and over either because the Enemy has us so focused on the situation, or because of our simple inability to fashion coherent thoughts or the words to express our petitions. It is then that we simply draw a circle of prayer and prostrate ourselves—physically or spiritually—before the throne of God. Charles John Ellicott, English Christian theologian and academic wrote of Romans 8:26 in his commentary:

> When the Christian's prayers are too deep and too intense for words, when they are rather a sigh heaved from the heart than any formal utterance, then we may know that they are prompted by the Spirit Himself. It is He who is praying to God for us.

Senior Pastor Carter Conlon, Times Square Church in New York City, wrote of this groaning prayer:

> God hears every cry, and every groan is a prayer. Every time you step out of your apartment or house and let out a sigh simply because you want God, that is a prayer. It is a cry for Him; it is a cry for His righteousness, His power, His glory and His ways. Everyone around you may be calling you weak in this hour, but ultimately you will be the one who is able to stand in the midst of the storm.

And we were certainly in the midst of a storm roiling with danger! Suddenly, we were startled by a rap on the car window. Despite my seeming bravado, I jumped at the sound. I thought, *This is it! We're going to meet our Maker out in the middle of nowhere. God help us!* Sometimes we become so focused on what to say or how to pray, we forget that God does not require prolific prayer or theological treatises. Michael J. Svigel, professor of Theological Studies at Dallas Theological Seminary wrote:

Christians can get hung up on method, worried that they haven't said the right words, haven't prayed hard or often enough, or haven't believed deeply enough. That's hocus-pocus, not prayer.

Standing at our car window was a young Arab man with his head covered by a *kaffiyeh*—the traditional head covering—and hefting not a weapon but a fuel can. First, I wondered how he could possibly have known our tank was empty. Second, I wondered from where he had come.

The man went to the back of the car, removed the cap, and poured fuel into the tank. He then walked over to the passenger door and pointed at the lock. I hesitated only briefly and then reached for the lock. He opened the door and climbed inside.

"Drive," he ordered. We had no idea where he was taking us. I looked in the rearview mirror at my passengers, shrugged, and complied. For thirty-two kilometers the young man did not speak another word, only pointed in the direction he wished the car to go. After what seemed like hours, he barked, "Stop." The man opened the door and climbed from the car. He slammed the door, stuck his head back inside, and said, "Safe."

I swiveled to look at my friends in the back seat—when I turned back, the young man was gone. We were out in the open. There was no mound of rocks for him to hide behind and no obvious way for him to have disappeared as quickly as he had. No one spoke a word until we drove over the border into Israel. One of my friends looked at me in awe and asked, "Can you explain what just happened?" I couldn't, other than that God answered the prayers for safety that had been prayed over us before we left Beirut.

An angel? I know the Bible says, "Do not forget to entertain strangers, for by so doing some have unwittingly entertained angels" (Hebrews 13:2). There was no doubt in my mind that God had sent an angel. There is no other way anyone could have known what we were facing; no way could an Arab man have shown up in the middle of the night with a can of fuel even as our vehicle was illuminated by spotlights and being targeted with small cannon fire. No possible way he could have been there one minute and gone the following.

As the Holy Spirit interceded for us, God provided for our deliverance in a miraculous way. We were lost in the desert when God intervened. Mark Batterson wrote of how we respond to God's detours in connection to the story of Balaam's donkey:

> We hate detours! They are frustrating. They are confusing. But the divine detours often get us where God wants us to go. The real miracle in this story isn't the talking donkey; the real miracle is a God who loves us enough to get in the way when we're going the wrong way. These are the miracles we don't want, but these are the miracles we need ... What seems like an unanswered prayer means that God has a better answer.

Those of us in that little car in the dead of night, stranded alone in the desert, quickly learned Jehovah-Jireh had a better way of escape—one that we would never forget.

And so I end this chapter as it began: "For He shall give His angels charge over you, to keep you in all your ways" (Psalm 91:11).

14

*Confess your offenses to one another,
and pray one for another, that you may be healed.
The effective, earnest prayer of a righteous man
is powerfully effective.*

—JAMES 5:16 HNV

During my early ministry, I was invited to go with beloved author, pastor, and friend Jamie Buckingham on a trek through the Sinai. When the invitation came in 1978 to accompany Jamie and a group of men on the trip of a lifetime, I was traveling through my own desert place and looked forward to leaving my cares behind to hike and fellowship for eleven days with that august group of men. The plan was to follow the footsteps of Moses from Jebel Musa in the southern Sinai to Al-Arish on the border of the Gaza Strip and Israel. We were scheduled to make side trips to other places Jamie had traveled.

Early on our trek, we stumbled upon a Bedouin encampment and stopped to visit with its inhabitants. An Arab woman came out to greet us. When she learned there was a doctor in our midst,

Dr. Angus Sargent, she ran into her tent and returned carrying what was probably a six-year-old daughter in her arms. We were appalled at the child's appearance. Flies covered a wound she'd received to her head and I could see, even from a distance, that the wound was badly infected. As the mother spoke and our guide interpreted, we learned that a family member had tried to cauterize the wound with a hot knife, which only made matters worse. My mind recoiled at the thought of the pain the child must have endured.

Angus examined her but after a moment shook his head. "I'm sorry. There's nothing I can do. I can't help her. She needs surgery, but we have no way or equipment to do that here."

As he said those words, a scripture from Isaiah came to mind. "But He was wounded for our transgressions, He was bruised for our iniquities; the chastisement for our peace was upon Him, and by His stripes we are healed" (Isaiah 53:5).

Remembering that passage, my heart was filled to overflowing with compassion for the child and her mother. When I looked at her, I thought of my three daughters back home in the United States. As a father, what would I be willing to do to see the needs of my daughters met?

Without hesitation, I held my hand over the girl's head and we circled her and joined in prayer, imploring God to heal the child as tears ran freely down our faces. I prayed in Hebrew and, as it and Arabic are similar, I hoped the mother understood at least some of what I said.

That was a special moment for us. The mother seemed genuinely glad that we had taken the time to listen and had responded as best we could. It was also a moment for me, too, as I realized that God had affirmed me once again, just as He had in my youth. This time by the words He'd given Isaiah long ago and by the prompting He'd placed in my spirit.

When we arose the next morning, Angus surprisingly announced, "I have to set up a makeshift operating room. I have to try to operate on that little girl. Otherwise she may not survive the infection." I didn't tell him what I'd sensed as we prayed for the girl the day before.

A few minutes later, Angus walked over to the mother's tent and not long after that we heard him crying. My heart sank at the thought that he must be mourning the child's death, so I eased open the tent flap and stepped inside to console him. Looking around, I saw the girl lying on a pile of rugs. Amazingly, the ugly wound from the day before was gone and the skin of her head was smooth and clear. She was completely healed!

When we finally walked from the tent, I raised my hands and lifted my eyes toward heaven. I realized that when I stopped complaining and got out of God's way, He was able to do the miraculous through me. How like us humans to try to do our own thing—to focus on self and our needs rather than on God, our Strength and our Redeemer!

Another experience the following day was not quite as awe-inspiring as the healing of the Bedouin girl. Like Moses, however, the lessons learned in the midst of desert places have certainly sustained me through the hard times. Honestly, waiting is hard. It seemed I had been taken aside and left there far too long. I struggled with what to do, when to do it, how to do it, where to go, and to whom to reach out. The previous day, the healing of the child had been uplifting and inspiring, but now what?

God had sidelined Moses in the desert and he had no idea how long he would be there, or if he would ever be allowed to return to the only home he had ever known in Egypt. Was I to experience the same feeling of abandonment?

Blogger Dr. Ken Matto wrote of lessons learned during desert experiences:

> While we are on the backside of the desert, God is not abandoning us but He is working out circumstances in our life. . . . if we respond correctly to our situation, then God has promised to guide us in all the judgments we make. . . . He will also teach us His way. One of the things He will definitely teach us is that our circumstances are tailor made for us and if we do not espouse an attitude of anger, then God will be able to teach us His ways. We may never know why He is doing something but we will learn something about the promises of God. I want you to try and picture two locations which would be about ten miles apart. We are at location number 1

which is us. Location number 2 is where God is now doing something which will eventually concern us. It is like the situation of Moses. Moses was tending sheep in Midian, while God was working out the circumstances for the greatest defeat of the most powerful nation on earth at that time, Egypt, but for those forty years that God was working in Egypt, Moses had no idea what was happening.

For him, one year turned into ten, twenty, thirty, thirty-nine until finally on one very special morning, Moses led the sheep to a place to graze. He had no idea that his life was about to change dramatically. Everything Jehovah had taught him in the desert would be needed for the next phase of his ministry to the Hebrew slaves held captive by Pharaoh. The man who had literally been plucked from the waters of adversity by the daughter of a king, and spared having been lunch for the crocodiles of the Nile, was about to need every skill he had learned as a shepherd. It was quite obvious to me in hindsight that God was trying to teach me patience—as I struggled to watch, wait, and follow Him.

Would I meet God in the middle of the desert as Moses had? Would there be a burning bush to illuminate my pathway? I wanted that feeling of being turned aside to experience something greater than myself, a miraculous sight. All the while, God wanted me to simply do what Moses had done; He wanted me to simply look to Him to be raised above my battle with depression and into the presence of my Savior.

Rather than being elevated to lofty heights, however, I was presented with my turn at doing kitchen duty. Kitchen police, or KP to us army veterans, had come much too soon for me. That morning after we had eaten our breakfast, I looked around but there were no dishwashers, farmhouse sinks, or even soap. Might I add: There was not much water, either? So there I was squatting beneath the brightening sky, dodging scorpions and scrubbing the pots and eating utensils with sand—the universal scouring pad. But rather than enjoying the opportunity to live like a Bedouin and being introduced to things few Westerners might ever get to experience, I complained. Just like the people of Israel who followed Moses into the wilderness. Not an auspicious start to my day!

I suppose I had forgotten for the moment what had happened to the complaining Israelites. As I likewise complained to God about my circumstances, I reached for my Bible. The pages fell open to the book of Numbers chapter fourteen, the chapter that records the murmuring and complaining Moses endured from his followers. It also records God's response, which was to send them wandering in the wilderness for forty years. I certainly didn't want that! Grudgingly, I closed my mouth and tried to enjoy the day's activities.

The next morning Jamie had made plans for the group to climb Mount Sinai and visit the spot where Aaron and Hur had held Moses' hands up for victory in the battle against the Amalekites:

> But Moses' hands became heavy; so they took a stone and put it under him, and he sat on it. And Aaron and Hur supported his hands, one on one side, and the other on the other side; and his hands were steady until the going down of the sun. —Exodus 17:12

Still full of myself, I decided to ignore the others and avoid the long hours trudging up the side of the mountain. I was a jogger; I could certainly make it to the top in much less time.

With merely a glance at the other trekkers, I left my extra gear behind—including my water bottle—discarded my shirt and took off running—straight up the path on the side of the mountain. When I reached the summit, instead of celebrating in victory I collapsed in a heap. By the time the rest of the team arrived, I was in the throes of heat exhaustion. I was sweating profusely, my pulse racing, my head pounding, and my muscles aching. I must have appeared weak and pale, and was definitely light-headed.

Rather than speaking up, I sat quietly and listened while Bill Nelson, a former astronaut, delivered a devotional on being one with Christ. By the time he finished I knew I was in trouble. I had no other option but to ask for help. "Bill," I croaked, "I'm sick. I need help." He kindly gave me his extra shirt and hat from his backpack, and then offered a few sips of water. Dr. Sargent diagnosed heat exhaustion, and after a time, I was finally able, with the help of my friends, to stagger back down the mountainside to our camp below, where I crawled into my tent and out of the burning rays of the desert sun.

That night, as I thought back over the events of the day, the accusing voices inside me returned, telling me what a stupid idea it had been—first, to run up the mountain alone, and second, to come on the trip at all. The desert wind and heat were unbearable. The scorpions and snakes were a real health hazard. It was awful out there and the wounded little kid inside me screamed, *Why me, God? Couldn't you find someone else to torment? How can I get out of this desert?*

Thinking again of the chapter in Numbers that I had read that morning, I bowed my head in prayer and confessed my complaining spirit to God. I admitted to Him that I was proud, stubborn, and rebellious, and neither did I like to submit to authority, which was the reason I had dashed up the mountain on my own in the first place. There in the desert, I drew a prayer circle around my attitude and laid it at the feet of the One who could help me be an overcomer. With that confession, the headache and fever that had bothered me all evening disappeared! God was trying to teach me to be totally submissive, humble, and obedient to Him.

During the years of wandering through the desert, not only was Moses obedient to the divine instructions given him, he was extraordinarily patient.

With perhaps a look back at that time in the desert, Jamie Buckingham wrote of the wilderness experience and its value:

> Learning to wait patiently, learning to do today what your hand finds to do, learning to hear the call of God when it comes, and to respond—that is what the wilderness is all about. Once a man submits his life to God's control, he voluntarily surrenders the right to determine or the power to vary the consequences of that decision. From that moment on, no situation can ever come into the life of the believer which has not first passed through the hands of God and thus has redeeming quality.

Moses had been called to lead a company of people that continually grumbled, complained, and finally mutinied. It was not surprising that eventually Moses' patience reached its breaking point, and in anger he failed to follow God's instructions (see Numbers 20). He disobeyed God at that one crucial juncture, showing a lack of trust in God's ability to provide, and his punishment was that he would not be allowed to enter into the promised land. Instead, that honor would belong to his successor, Joshua. However, God *did* take Moses to the top of the mountain and allow him to see the other side—the land that flowed with milk and honey. Then Moses died and the Lord buried him. As we read in Deuteronomy 34:5–6:

> So Moses the servant of the LORD died there in the land of Moab, according to the word of the LORD. And He buried him in a valley in the land of Moab, opposite Beth Peor; but no one knows his grave to this day.

Despite missteps, Moses' life was characterized by obedience. He led a nation of rebellious, dissatisfied, disobedient, quarrelsome, and complaining people through the wilderness to the banks of the Jordan River. Through all the ups and downs, the years of wandering in the desert, Moses held high the name of Jehovah-Nissi—God our Banner. It was a banner of encouragement "to give you a future and a hope" (Jeremiah 29:11b).

Moses was able to defeat the forces of the Enemy because he was submissive to God's will. He delivered his people from the chains of darkness and degradation because he complied with Jehovah's instructions. Moses' obedience and trust won him unfailing favor with God and he was called a "friend of God."

15

Our Father which art in heaven, Hallowed be thy name.

MATTHEW 6:9 KJV

In the entire New Testament, Jesus taught His disciples only one prayer; some today refer to it as the Lord's Prayer. Though many of us recite it from memory in services or on occasions where various denominations gather, how often do we really think about its significance or expect this prayer to actually be answered? Let's look at it for a moment and think about praying it as if you were melding with the words of the prayer and, more importantly, with Jehovah to see His will accomplished on the earth:

> Our Father which art in heaven, Hallowed be thy name. Thy kingdom come, Thy will be done in earth, as it is in heaven. Give us this day our daily bread. And forgive us our debts, as we forgive our debtors. And lead us not into temptation, but deliver us from evil: For thine is the kingdom, and the power, and the glory, for ever. Amen.

Author Jan Karon wrote a series of books about a vicar in the fictional village of Mitford. The main character was often heard to pray what he called "the prayer that never fails." During her various books about the pastor and his congregation, we learn that prayer was, "Thy will be done."

Ben Helmer, vicar at St. James' Parish in Eureka Springs, Arkansas, wrote of the efficacy of this particular prayer:

> First, when we make our specific prayer we do so from our finite human perspective, but God's mind is infinite and he sees things we cannot. Second, God's will is for the good of all who love him (Rom. 8:28). He is not mean. His will is always best for us even when we do not understand. Third, when we pray this way we are reminded that God always answers our prayers. He just does not always answer the way we think he should! Finally, it reminds us not to pray without considering the plans and wishes of the Lord.
>
> So pray for every detail, but don't forget that your Father in heaven always knows best. Whether you say the words or not, be sure your attitude is such that you seek His purpose in yours prayers. Then, in your darkest moments, you can pray the perfect prayer that never fails.

This very simple yet profound prayer says:

- ✧ our Father—Abba—Jesus opens the door for an intimate relationship with God;

- ✧ I worship and praise You;

- ✧ I want Your kingdom to be realized on earth just as it is in heaven;

- ✧ I will trust in Your provision;

- ✧ I will forgive others as You have forgiven me;

- ✧ through Your strength I will resist temptation and avoid evil;

- ✧ because You are the owner of the kingdom, power, and glory that will last forever;

- ✧ Amen or "so let it be."

Everything that is encompassed in being a Christian is in this prayer, and the main purpose of being a Believer is right there at the beginning: "Thy kingdom come. They will be done in earth, as it is in heaven."

Author, pastor, and theologian Dr. Charles Swindoll wrote:

> Prayer was never intended to make us feel guilty. It was never intended as a verbal marathon for only the initiated. Real prayer—the kind of prayer that Jesus mentioned and modeled—is realistic, spontaneous, down-to-earth communication with the living Lord that results in a relief of personal anxiety and a calm assurance that our God is in full control of our circumstances.

The true purpose of the church—the body of Christ on Earth today—is simply to see His will done here as it is in heaven.

Look for a moment at what Jesus said the kingdom of heaven is like:

1. A grain of mustard seed—it may start as the smallest of all things, but when it is planted and grows, it becomes a place of shelter, lodging, and protection (see Matthew 13:31–32).

2. Yeast—though it is only added to a small part of something, it will soon permeate and change everything with which it comes in contact (see Matthew 13:33).

3. A hidden treasure and a pearl of great price—for the joy of having this one thing, a person would be willing to sell everything else they own to possess it (see Matthew 13:44–46), and those who trust in their wealth and possessions rather than in God will have a hard time entering into it (see Mark 10:23–26).

4. A net—which when it is cast in the sea will return full to the boat with every kind of fish (see Matthew 13:47–50).

5. A man hiring workers for his vineyard and a king inviting guests to his son's wedding—those who come to it will receive its reward whether they come early or late, and though many are invited, only those who answer that call will enjoy its benefits: "For many are called, but few are chosen" (see Matthew 20:1–16 and 22:2–14).

Jesus told us we should pray that His kingdom be ushered in on earth as in heaven. This is what the earthly church meant to do—shepherd His kingdom. How can we possibly do this if we truly do not know Him or are not one with Him?

Jesus gave a simple illustration of this to His disciples. I think most of us tend to miss a nuance of this teaching that would help to clarify this. Please read the following passage in Matthew 18:1–4 carefully and prayerfully:

> At the same time came the disciples unto Jesus, saying, Who is the greatest in the kingdom of heaven? And Jesus called a little child unto him, and set him in the midst of them, and said, Verily I say unto you, Except ye be converted, and *become as little children*, ye shall not enter into the kingdom of heaven. Whosoever therefore shall humble himself *as this little child*, the same is greatest in the kingdom of heaven. (KJV, italics added)

Many have read this story before, or have even heard a sermon or two on the passage. We may have come away with the message that we should be like little children before God if we want to enter His kingdom. We have centered on the point that we should have the attributes of children—innocence, trustfulness, simplicity, obedience—as the central meaning of this passage. This is certainly an important part of it, *but it is not necessarily the answer to the disciples' question*. Reread the passage and you will see Jesus' response is twofold: (1) except that you become as *a* little child, you shall not enter the kingdom of heaven, and (2) whoever shall humble himself as *this* little child shall become the greatest in the kingdom of heaven.

Jesus is being very specific here in this second point: It is not the general principle of childlikeness alone that ushers us into living God's kingdom on earth today, but there is something special about *this one child* that will teach us great things about living in God's kingdom. Was it who the child was? Was he some saint that would do great things later in life? Was Jesus showing His disciples someone they should look to for guidance later after Jesus was gone?

The passage gives us no suggestion of this. In fact, the key concept Jesus was teaching is plainly in what He said: "Whosoever therefore shall humble himself as (or like) this little child . . ." The point was not in *who* the child was, but *in what the child did*. How did he humble himself? *He simply did what Jesus asked without question or hesitation.*

Picture the scene again: The disciples ask Jesus a question, and in response Jesus turns around and sees a little boy walking by, perhaps carrying grain for his parents or on some other task, or perhaps even simply running down the street playing with some friends. Jesus says, "Child," catching the boy's attention, "come here." The boy stops whatever he is doing, however important his errand, or however much he may have been enjoying his play, and walks over to Jesus in obedience. He didn't say, "Sure, Jesus, just as soon as I finish what I am doing." Nor did he say, "Aw, come on, can't I finish my game first?" No, he goes immediately without saying a word. Then Jesus takes the boy lovingly by the shoulders, faces him toward the disciples and says, "Whosoever shall humble himself *as* this little child, the same is greatest in the kingdom of heaven."

This is what I have experienced again and again in my life, though more often by accident than intent. At times when I was completely dependent upon God, knowing I could do nothing in my own strength, stripped of all self-confidence, my desperate prayer would be, "God, if You don't do it, it can't be done." Then I simply did what God told me to do in response. I had no idea that my desperate heart's cry was the fertile soil in which the glory of God could be manifested.

Now I see clearly that those times when Jesus has moved the most powerfully were when I leaned the most heavily upon Him. Whenever He has moved mightily was when "I" moved out. Jesus would show up and softly speak, and when I obeyed, I would see His will done on the earth as if we were actually standing before His throne in heaven. This is receiving the kingdom of God like a child.

It is through those who have spent time with Jesus, who commune with Him through prayer and reading the Word, who obey His voice, that His kingdom becomes real on earth.

If *each* of us would just be one with Jesus, then *all* of us would have no problem working together in the earth to bring forth His kingdom.

David wrote of it in this way:

> Behold, how good and how pleasant it is for brethren to dwell together in unity! It is like the precious ointment upon the head, that ran down upon the beard, even Aaron's beard: that went down to the skirts of his garments; as the dew of Hermon, and as the dew that descended upon the mountains of Zion: for there the LORD commanded the blessing, even life for evermore.
> —Psalm 133 KJV

According to *Vine's Expository Dictionary*, the word *together* here "emphasizes a plurality in unity. In some contexts the connotation is on community in action." Here, David is saying that the place where brothers and sisters work together is this kind of unity. It is the place of God's anointing! It is a place where we are refreshed and strengthened by God's Spirit as the dew nourishes the grass. It is the place where God *commands* blessing! And it is the place where *zoe*—the eternal, God-kind of life—flows freely!

Only when self is subjugated to Christ will we be one with God—and each other—to have this kind of unity. We will never be one by trying to agree with each other and putting aside differences of belief for the sake of unity alone. We are to be one as Jesus and His Father are one. Only when Jesus is on the throne in each of our lives can we be in tune with His purpose and be one Body on earth able to work corporately to bring true and lasting revival. Only when self is subjugated to Jesus will His "greater works" flourish as the body of Christ grows into His fullness and carries forth His kingdom on the earth.

This is what atonement—"at-one-ment"—is all about: we must be at one with Jesus. This unity can only be achieved through communion with Him. Andrew Murray, the late South African evangelist and author, wrote:

> Who can say what power a church could develop and exercise if it gave itself to the work of prayer day and night for God's power on His servants and His word, and for the glorifying of God in the salvation of souls? Most churches think their members are gathered into one simply to take care of and build up each other. They do not know that God rules the world by the prayers of His saints, that prayer is the power by which Satan is conquered, that by prayer the Church on earth has at its disposal the powers of the heavenly world. They do not remember that Jesus has, by His promise, consecrated every assembly in His Name to be a gate of heaven, where His Presence is to be felt, and His Power experienced in the Father fulfilling their desires.

Matthew 21:12–13 (ESV) reminds us of Jesus' reaction to finding the temple courts filled with those whose only thought appeared to be materialism:

> And Jesus entered the temple and drove out all who sold and bought in the temple, and he overturned the tables of the money-changers and the seats of those who sold pigeons. He said to them, "It is written, 'My house shall be called a house of prayer,' but you make it a den of robbers."

What prompted Jesus to make such an uncompromising statement? He was in Jerusalem for Passover, the most sacred of all Jewish feasts. Jesus looked about with what must have been great dismay; His Father's house was rife with the greediness of the money changers and merchants who had taken up residence in the temple court. Dr. John MacArthur, pastor and theologian, wrote:

> As He surveyed the sacred temple grounds now turned into a bazaar, Jesus was appalled and outraged. The worshipful atmosphere that befitted the temple, as the symbol of God's presence, was completely absent. What should have been a place of sacred reverence and adoration had become a place of abusive commerce and excessive overpricing. The sound of heartfelt praise and fervent prayers had been drowned out by the bawling of oxen, the bleating of sheep, the cooing of doves, and the loud haggling of vendors and their customers.

No longer was Jehovah at the center of temple worship; a disease had taken center stage in God's house: the cancer of greed.

In the days leading up to Passover, many merchants had set up their shops outside Jerusalem on the roads leading into the city. Once the majority of the pilgrims had arrived, the hawkers moved into the temple court to ply their trade. Among the sellers were those who supplied pigeons to the poor, the lowliest of all sacrifices allowed by the law. The problem was that the price for a common bird was so exorbitant the poor could not afford it as an offering, leaving them empty-handed.

Into the center of this maelstrom of greed taking place in His Father's house walked the Son of God, filled with righteous indignation. Such zeal had brought Him, early in His ministry, on a collision course with evil and those who practiced it. Not having learned the lesson about which we read in John 2, one that Jesus had taught early in His ministry, the money changers and vendors returned to the temple during the Passover celebration.

Author and teacher Charles Swindoll wrote of Jesus' response:

> Very often, people portray Jesus as the meek and mild teacher who taught His followers to love others as themselves, to avoid retaliation by turning the other cheek, to pursue peace, and to avoid judging others. While Jesus did indeed possess these qualities and teach these values, the picture is incomplete. These passages

reveal that Jesus was more than the pale, languid figure often portrayed in art, on television, and in movies.

John (2:17) concludes his record of this event with, "Then His disciples remembered that it was written, 'Zeal for Your house has eaten Me up'" (see Psalm 69:9). The fervor of Jesus for His Father's house was not anger based; His response was not fueled by rage or resentment. No, His zeal was a holy protectiveness, a heavenly love for the earthly sign of God's presence, the symbol of His purpose, and a place of unhindered prayer. It was there that the Israelites, His people, were to go to pray and to worship Jehovah. It was there they were to hear the words of the patriarchs, poets, and prophets. It was there in the house of God that reverence was to be the order of the day. Jesus did not respond in rage or foolhardiness, but with righteous indignation.

Why might this have been such a point of contention for Jesus? Pastor Eric Lenhart of North Main Street Church of God in Butler, Pennsylvania, proffered this explanation:

> The court of the Gentiles was the outer most court in the area of the Temple where only the gentiles, the handicapped, and the unclean could come to pray and worship. With all the activity of a common-day market place, there was no way that worship and prayer could be offered in such a place as this. With sheep bleating, coins jingling, doves cooing, and people sputtering deals

to acquire a sacrifice from the merchants, the worshipers were inevitably crowded out.... Jesus gave to those who would have otherwise been left by the wayside by those going into the inner courts to worship and pray; those more privileged to come closer to the Holy of Holies than they. And this is the true nature and character of God: always giving, always loving, always extending a hand of grace and forgiveness to those who honestly seek him.

The religious leaders and teachers of the law had forgotten God's true character. They had become so wrapped up in the legalities of the law, so puffed up by the pursuit of power and position, that they worshiped the structure of everyday life rather than the Giver of true life.

We must never take for granted the price that was paid for our privilege of entering into the presence of a holy, living God—the opportunity to make our requests known to the Ruler of the Universe.

16

Behold, how good and how pleasant it is for brethren to dwell together in unity!
It is like the precious oil upon the head, running down on the beard,
the beard of Aaron, running down on the edge of his garments.
It is like the dew of Hermon, descending upon the mountains of Zion;
for there the Lord commanded the blessing—life forevermore.

—PSALM 133

Following Israel's rebirth, organizations in support of the return of the Jewish people to the Holy Land began to spring up—many comprised of Bible-believing Christians. By the late twentieth century, Evangelical ranks had been infused with ever-growing numbers of those God-fearing people who bless Israel in daily prayer and intercession as well as with monetary support. Many are members of groups whose focus is on biblical promises made by God to Abraham and his descendants. Among them are the Jerusalem Prayer Team, Friends of Zion Heritage Center, and Churches United with Israel.

The members of these organizations have great respect for the Jewish people and for Judaism. They believe this is the very foundation upon which Christianity is based—after all, Jesus was a Jew who kept the Mosaic law.

A Jerusalem Prayer Team–sponsored petition to President George W. Bush in 2003 read in part:

> We support Israel's right to their land spiritually and legally. History records that God deals with nations in accord with how these nations deal with Israel. We rejoice that here in America, for 228 years, we have been committed to the Jewish people. The Jewish people have found refuge here; they have found a people who love them; and we can take pride in saying that Israel is not an exclusively Jewish issue.
>
> Bible-believing Evangelicals consider the support of Israel a biblical mandate. Regardless of contrary opinion, we do not believe Israel has to offer an excuse for its existence. Israel lives today as a right! A right that has been hallowed by the Bible, by history, by sacrifice, by prayer, and by the yearning for peace!

Multitudes believe God's promise to Abraham: Those who bless His descendants will be blessed of God (see Genesis 12:3).

In 1982, I sponsored the first National Prayer Breakfast in honor of Israel. A "Proclamation of Blessing" was introduced in support of the Jewish nation. It stated:

> As Bible-believing Americans, we believe there exists an ironclad bond between the State of Israel and

the United States. We believe that bond to be a moral imperative.

Representing the vast majority of evangelicals in the United States, we have gathered together at this National Prayer Breakfast to reaffirm our support and prayers, that this bond not be weakened or diminished.

Another God-directed initiative was the purchase and restoration of Corrie ten Boom's family home in Haarlem, Holland. It has become a lighthouse that beams forth the love of true Christians for God's chosen people. It reveals the depths to which the Ten Boom family went in order to save Jewish people during the Holocaust, or in Hebrew, *Ha Shoah* (the catastrophe).

On May 10, 1940, the people of Holland came face-to-face with the reality of war: Germany invaded their country, which had hoped to remain neutral. Earlier in the evening, the Ten Boom family had gathered around Casper's prized radio to hear the Dutch prime minister address the country. He assured the people that there was nothing to fear. Casper was incensed by these comments, and proclaimed, "It is wrong to give people hope when there is no hope. It is wrong to base faith upon wishes. There will be war. The Germans will attack, and we will fall."

Her father's prophecy came to pass one night as he and his family were in bed asleep. Suddenly the jarring sound of explosions rent the air. Corrie bolted upright and grabbed her robe. Slipping her arms into the sleeves, she raced downstairs, paused outside her father's room, and hearing only the sounds of his whiffling snores, moved on to her older sister Betsie's room. Corrie felt her way across the bedroom to find Betsie, who was sitting upright in the darkness. The two sisters embraced and said in unison, "War."

Weeks later, awakening to sounds of airplanes engaged in dogfights roaring overhead, Corrie had slipped downstairs to the kitchen for a cup of tea with Betsie. Suddenly an explosion rocked the dishes in the cupboards. Soon, the noise died away and both young women climbed the stairs back to bed. Corrie felt for the edge of her bed and her hand closed over something hard and metallic. She felt an ooze of blood down her finger. She raced back downstairs with a 10-inch piece of metal shrapnel clutched in her hand. It had penetrated the roof of the Ten Boom home. As her sister tended her cut hand, Corrie was aghast at the implications of what she had found and the "what ifs" had she been asleep in her bed. Betsie soothed her fears with:

> There are no "ifs" in God's world. And no places that are safer than other places. The center of His will is our only safety—O Corrie, let us pray that we may always know it.

None of the family could foresee the devastating events that were slowly but inexorably creeping over their homeland.

One night, shortly thereafter, the sisters were kneeling in prayer when Corrie experienced what she could only later describe as a vision. In this vision, she, Betsie, their father, brother Willem, nephew Peter, and a number of strangers were being driven through the square in Haarlem in the back of a wagon. To her horror, they were unable to climb down from the dray that was carrying them farther and farther from their home. She cried out in horror and told Betsie about the vision. Betsie reassured Corrie, "If God has shown us bad times ahead, it's enough for me that He knows about them. That's why He sometimes shows us things, you know—to tell us that this too is in His hands."

Five days later the news came that Holland had surrendered and Queen Wilhelmina had fled to England. Over the next months, the Dutch people gradually became aware of the horrors of anti-Semitism. At first, it was negligible—a rock through a window or slurs painted like ugly slashes across synagogue walls and on the front doors of Jewish homes. Jews were denied service in restaurants, libraries, theaters, and other gathering places. Finally, patches in the shape of six-pointed yellow stars were handed out that by law had to be worn prominently on clothing, each bearing the word *Jood* (Jew). Then Jews began to silently disappear, as if they had never existed.

On one of their walks, Corrie and her father saw Jews in the public square being loaded like so many cattle into the back of a truck—men, women, and children—all bearing the ignominious yellow star. Corrie wept for the people; Casper pitied the Germans, for, he said, they were "touching the apple of God's eye."

Biographer Norman Grubb wrote of theologian and prayer warrior Rees Howells' burden for a group of Jewish children at the beginning of World War II. The commentary was dated September 11, 1938:

> The moment I read this [that Hitler had thrown out several thousand Jewish children on the Polish border], a great anguish came over me. Nobody knows what this must mean to their parents. The Holy Spirit is ~~just like~~ a father, and if I were a father of children whose home had been destroyed, wouldn't I seek shelter for them straight away? The Holy Spirit suffers like that for all those parents on the Continent. Unless He in you makes the suffering your own, you can't intercede for them. You will never touch the Throne unless you send up that real cry; words don't count at all. — *They do - it's the heart that counts.*

It was Corrie's nephew Kik, Willem's son, who was responsible for helping put feet to some of the prayers sent heavenward behalf of the Jews of Holland. He was instrumental in helping the Weils, the Ten Booms' neighbors across the street, escape the Nazi threat, and who first placed the thought in her mind of working with the Underground. Once the seed was planted, God began to water it and cultivate it until, on May 10, 1942, the seedling burst forth into the light, and the lives of the Ten Boom family were forever changed. (Kik died in the Bergen-Belsen Concentration Camp. He was incarcerated for aiding a downed American pilot.)

The edict had been handed down from Nazi headquarters that the singing of the Dutch national anthem "Wilhelmus" was *verboten* (forbidden). Corrie, Betsie, and Casper were on their way to attend Sunday services at the Dutch Reformed Church in Velsen, a small town nearby. The German occupation had been responsible for one good thing in Holland: Churches were filled to overflowing with worshipers. Peter, another nephew, had been selected as church organist in a competition of forty entrants. When they arrived, Peter was in the organ loft, hidden from the crowd below. As the service concluded, the crowd emitted a unified gasp; Peter had pulled out all the stops on the huge organ and was playing the "Wilhelmus" at full volume. Casper ten Boom was the first to rise to his feet until finally the entire congregation joined in singing the outlawed national anthem.

Peter was clearly a hero to the burdened Dutch people, but Corrie worried that he might be arrested for his forbidden but victorious organ recital. For several days his safety seemed secure, but then his little sister, Cocky, burst into the clock shop to inform everyone that Peter had been arrested and taken away to the federal prison in Amsterdam. For two months he would languish in a cold, dark concrete cell at the prison before being released. He was thinner, paler, but not the least bit intimidated by his arrest.

Two weeks later, the Ten Boom family home became a way station on the Underground Railroad, which aided Jews in escaping the Nazis. Just before evening curfew a knock summoned Corrie to the alley door. There stood a heavily veiled woman. When Corrie opened the door, the woman stepped inside and identified herself as a Jew seeking asylum. Casper welcomed her and explained that all of God's children were welcome in his home. Two nights later, another furtive knock sounded at the side door. An elderly couple stood there, also seeking asylum.

The following day, Corrie traveled to seek Willem's advice. As he talked with Corrie on how to procure ration cards, she thought of a friend who worked in the Food Office. With the help of Fred Koornstra, Corrie was able to surreptitiously secure enough ration cards to feed the Jewish refugees who passed through the Ten Boom home.

The secret room or "The Hiding Place," as it would later become known, was the brainchild of one of Europe's most respected architects, whom they knew only as Mr. Smit. (Many of the underground workers were labeled "Smit." This made it difficult for other workers to identify these brave volunteers.) This elderly wisp of a man freely gave of his time and energy to design and direct workmen who built a room so secure and unidentifiable that the Gestapo failed to ever find it. A signal was devised to indicate that it was safe to enter the Ten Boom home. This was an Alpina Watches sign that was hung in the dining room window.

Once the room was completed, "guests" rehearsed getting into the hiding place quickly until they could vacate the lower floors and move safely inside the compartment in less than two minutes. Corrie practiced stalling techniques to delay anyone who might come in search of the hidden Jews. One of their guests, Leendert, a schoolteacher, even installed an alarm system that would sound an early warning if unwanted visitors threatened.

Since the Ten Boom home was situated near the center of Haarlem, Corrie worked diligently to secure other hiding places for the people who might enter the clock shop for help. She enlisted farmers, owners of large homes, and others who wanted to give aid to the tormented Jewish population. She amassed a group of about eighty people, some of whom were teenagers, willing to risk their lives to carry coded messages between Corrie and her contacts. One such message read:

> We have a man's watch here that's giving us trouble.
> We can't find anyone to repair it. For one thing, the face
> is very old-fashioned.

That was translated as, "an elderly Jew whose facial features would give him away." This was a most difficult individual to place in a safe house. The Ten Boom family took him in and provided a haven for him.

Rolf, a local policeman who had provided aid to the Ten Boom family, stopped at the clock shop one afternoon. He had information that the Gestapo was going to raid a local safe house that night. Corrie summoned Jop, a seventeen-year-old volunteer, and asked him to deliver a message about the planned raid. Unfortunately for Jop, the Gestapo had already swooped down on the home and was lying in wait for the unsuspecting young man. He was quickly arrested and transported to the prison in Amsterdam. When Rolf returned with the news of Jop's arrest, members of the Ten Boom family were convinced they should stop their underground activities, but they refused to abandon their Jewish friends. Their work had to continue.

Corrie had taken to her bed for two days with influenza when, on February 28, 1944, a man claiming to need help to rescue his wife from prison came to the clock shop and demanded to speak only to her. Corrie painfully rose from her bed, dressed, and went downstairs. The visitor pleaded for 600 guilders in order to bribe a policeman and secure his wife's release. She arranged for the money, sent the man on his way, and slowly climbed back up the stairs to her sickbed. Sometime later she heard the incessant buzzing of the alarm system.

Corrie supposed just another drill was in progress—but that was soon followed by the realization that this was no drill. She heard the sound of boots tromping through the downstairs and heavy footfalls on the stairs below her room. She secured the trapdoor to the hiding place, set her "prison bag" in front of the panel, and dove back into her bed, feigning sleep.

The door to her room burst open and a tall, heavyset man demanded her name. "Cornelia ten Boom," she replied sleepily. The Gestapo leader, Kapteyn, demanded that she rise and dress. He casually asked, "So, where are you hiding the Jews?" Corrie denied any knowledge of Jews or an underground ring. He watched as Corrie pulled her clothes on over her pajamas, and with a regretful glance at her bag, which she had stuffed with necessities in case of capture, turned and walked out of the bedroom. She was prodded down the stairs into the kitchen, only to see that a uniformed soldier stood there. In the front room, Corrie was pleased to see the Alpina Watches sign lying smashed on the floor. Anyone walking past the shop would know it was not safe to enter its doors.

Another member of the Gestapo led Corrie into a separate room to be interrogated. Again and again she was asked to reveal the suspected secret room. Each time she refused she was struck repeatedly, but she still refused to answer, although she could taste the metallic tang of blood in her mouth. She cried, "Lord Jesus, help me." Her captor threatened to kill her if she spoke that name again, but he did stop the beating and eventually led her back to the room where her other family members were being held.

Corrie was shoved inside, and Betsie was led from the room. Corrie dropped into a chair and heard sounds of wood splintering as cupboard doors were smashed in search of the suspected hiding place. One German was sifting through the treasures that had been secreted in a corner cupboard on a lower floor. As the architect of the hidden room had predicted, it was the first place the Gestapo would look in their search for Jews. The destruction continued for another half hour, yet no secret room was found. When Betsie returned to the room where the other family members were being held, she was bleeding and bruised but had kept silent during the interrogation.

17

The glory of the young is their strength;
the gray hair of experience is the splendor of the old.

—Proverbs 20:29 NLT

Casper ten Boom, Corrie's frail eighty-four-year-old father, was arrested and dragged from his home along with his family to the local police station. He, too, was eventually taken to Scheveningen prison, where he was forced to sit for hours on a cold stone floor. The patriarch and Christian Zionist met evil face-to-face on that bitter February day in 1944. According to the Gestapo, he was guilty and worthy of death for one reason and one reason only: He was suspected of having helped Dutch Jews evade arrest and deportation to Adolf Hitler's concentration camps.

At the garrison a group of about thirty people waited in agony, wondering if they were destined to be executed before the sun rose the following day. One by one, they were questioned and their fate determined—some were released, while others were sent back to the confines of the airless hallway to continue in fearful suspense.

As darkness fell, a group of the frightened and disheartened gathered around Casper like children flocking to a beloved grandfather. Not able to encircle all of them with his arms, he embraced them with his voice as he quoted words from the Psalms that had for so long signified life and health to him: "Thou art my hiding place and my shield: I hope in thy word. . . . Hold thou me up, and I shall be safe" (Psalm 119:114, 117 KJV). His prayer was a benediction some would never again hear. As he quoted those beloved scriptures from memory, the group was comforted by their elder who shepherded them through those dark days. His unwavering faith would give them renewed strength.

Finally an official shouted, "Casper ten Boom!" The old man struggled to stand on his arthritic legs, riddled with pinpricks from the lack of circulation. He stumbled toward the door and was hustled inside the interrogation room, where he was cross-examined again. Calmly and confidently, peacefully and politely, the old grandfather painstakingly answered the questions barked at him. The inquisitor leaned back in his chair and, in one last effort to seize control over the self-disciplined octogenarian, smiled charmingly. Like the proposition Satan made to Christ in the desert, the Gestapo leader sat forward and smugly offered, "Old man, if you promise us you will not save any more Jews we will let you sleep in your own bed." Smiling the peaceful smile of the redeemed, Casper responded quietly, "I would consider it an honor to give my life for God's chosen people."

Even as they had been escorted from their home, their sanctuary, Corrie realized her earlier vision was about to become a reality: She and her family were being arrested, placed in a wagon, and would eventually be transported to an undetermined place from which they could not escape. They were taken first to the local police station and placed in the care of their friend Rolf. For the remainder of the day, they were forced to sit on the cold, hard floor of a large room with thirty-five members of their terrified underground family.

Rolf entered the room, spoke briefly to Willem, and then bellowed that there were toilets available that could be used under escort. After he left the room, Willem whispered to Corrie that this would be an opportunity for those inside to dispose of any papers they did not want to fall into the hands of the Gestapo.

The following morning the prisoners were loaded into buses and taken to the Scheveningen prison in The Hague, then just a small town about twenty-four miles south of Haarlem. When they disembarked, one of the guards pointed at Corrie's father and yelled, "Did you have to arrest that old man?" Willem led his father up to the check-in desk. The head of the prison peered into Casper's eyes and said, "I'd like to send you home. I'll take your word that you won't cause any more trouble."

Those standing nearby clearly heard his reply, "If I go home today, tomorrow I will open my door again to any man in need who knocks." As the group was led to their individual cells, none knew it would be the last time they would see Casper. On March 10, 1944,

Casper ten Boom died at The Hague Municipal Hospital after ten days of incarceration in the Scheveningen prison.

Casper's dedication and determination to assist God's chosen people came as the result of his father, Willem, having taken up the banner passed down to him by his great-grandfather, a Christian Zionist, who had begun a weekly meeting to pray for the peace of Jerusalem (Psalm 122:6) in 1844. Casper continued the meetings, where the family and others gathered specifically in prayer for the Jewish people. The meetings abruptly ended on February 28, 1944, when Nazi soldiers came to the house to take the family away.

Corrie's first prison assignment was a narrow cell, shared with four other women. When the matron determined that Corrie was quite ill, she was transported to the hospital. The doctor diagnosed her with pre-tuberculosis, hoping that she would be allowed to stay in the hospital. It was not to be; Corrie was taken back to the prison, but not before one of the nurses had slipped her a small packet containing soap, safety pins, and four individual booklets containing the Gospels.

Corrie gradually recovered from the influenza and began to wonder what had happened to the other people from Haarlem who had been transported to the prison. On Hitler's birthday, April 20, she had the opportunity to gather information about her family members and neighbors. While the wardens celebrated, the prisoners were able to shout back and forth to each other and gather yearned-for knowledge of loved ones. She learned that her sister Betsie was still at Scheveningen, that Willem had been released, and that Nollie had been discharged almost a month before. It would be much later before Corrie sadly learned of her father's death.

Shortly after the celebration, the door to Corrie's cell cracked open and a package landed with a thump on the floor. She was overjoyed to discover that it was from Nollie. Inside, she found a light blue embroidered sweater. It was like being enfolded in the comfort of Nollie's distant arms. The package also contained cookies, vitamins, a needle and thread, and a bright red towel.

As Corrie wrapped the items back up in the brown parcel paper, she noticed a discrepancy in the return address. Carefully removing the stamp, she found a joyous message: "All the watches in your closet are safe." Corrie rejoiced; all six of the Jews her family had been hiding had safely escaped the secret room. This, no doubt, helped her through the following four long months in solitary confinement, where her only contact was a lone ant that had found its way into her cell. She was grateful to God for friendship with even one of His smallest creatures. She shared crumbs from her daily ration of bread with the tiny insect.

Corrie knew that eventually she would face a hearing at the hands of the Gestapo interrogator. Finally, on a cool May morning, she was summoned from her tiny room. She was led through a labyrinth of halls and a courtyard sparkling with the drizzle of rain before entering one of the huts where the hearings were held. As she awaited her fate, she prayed, "Lord Jesus, You were called to a hearing too. Show me what to do."

The inquisitor, Lieutenant Rahms, noticed that Corrie was shivering from the cold, so he built a fire in the stove. He drew a chair forward, motioned for Corrie to sit, and very gently began to question his prisoner. For the next hour he probed, feinted, and parried in a macabre dance to gain Corrie's trust and glean information from his affection-starved detainee. He began, "I would like to help you, Miss ten Boom, but you must tell me everything."

Corrie was glad that among the drills practiced in her home in Haarlem was one of answering questions if captured by the Gestapo. Her training stood her in good stead. The officer questioned her about the ration cards and how they were obtained. She was relieved that she had no knowledge of how they had been provided. When asked about her other activities Corrie launched into a description of her work with the girls' clubs and the mentally disabled. The lieutenant seemed to have no understanding of why she found that so rewarding.

Rahms chided her for her waste of time with the disabled. Corrie responded, "God loves everyone, even the weak and feeble. The Bible says that God looks at things very differently from us." The officer abruptly ended the session and sent Corrie back to her cell. From that time forward, as long as Corrie was in Scheveningen, the lieutenant helped her as much as possible. He arranged for her to be allowed to see her family, using the pretext of the reading of Casper ten Boom's will. While they were all together, Willem slipped Corrie a compact Bible secreted in a pouch that she could wear around her neck.

Although the lieutenant could supply aid, he unfortunately did not have the authority to allow her and Betsie to return home. Nevertheless, Corrie spent time reading the precious Gospels that had been smuggled to her. She rejoiced that Jesus' death, though meant for evil, brought forgiveness to all who accepted His gift. She prayed that God would use her troubles to bring good to someone.

All those years later, thankful that God had spared this dear woman in Ravensbrück, Corrie and I enjoyed a bowl of soup together in a hotel restaurant in Texarkana, Texas, and shared our love for the Jewish people. It was Corrie's vision that her home and the clock shop in Haarlem, Holland, be restored.

18

Ask, and it will be given to you; seek, and you will find; knock, and it will be opened to you.

—MATTHEW 7:7

Later, after her death, I thought of Corrie's dream during those terrible war years, and by faith flew to the Netherlands to visit the clock shop and follow God's leading. As I walked around the shop, I asked about seeing the upstairs, where a total of eight hundred Jews had been hidden and saved during the Holocaust. The owner advised me that the door was kept locked, as the area was only used for storage. My heart broke. I felt that the Ten Boom clock shop should be open as a testimony to the world of the love of a Christian family for the Jewish people. As I stepped through the door onto the sidewalk, I prayed, "Lord, I want to buy this house and restore it. If it is Your will, please help me." That evening, I drew a prayer circle around my desire to fulfill Corrie's wishes. Knowing that Psalm 91 was her chapter of promise, I opened my Bible and read:

> He that dwelleth in the secret place of the most High shall abide under the shadow of the Almighty. I will say of the Lord, He is my refuge and my fortress: my God; in him will I trust. —Psalm 91:1–2 KJV

The next morning I awoke confident in God's answer. I returned to the clock shop and asked the owner if he would sell the shop to me. Just as he refused my offer, the clocks in the shop began to chime the noon hour. He turned to me and asked if I knew what day it was. I mentioned the day of the week. "No," he said. "That is not what I meant—today is April 15, Corrie's birthday. In her honor, yes, I will sell the shop to you."

When the sale was complete, I vowed that no one would ever pay a cent to visit the Ten Boom home—that the story of God's love would be available to all. Since its restoration was completed, the clock shop has been open, free of charge, to thousands of visitors. Many leave with tears of remembrance and grateful hearts for the family that gave their lives to help Jewish people escape Hitler's plan from hell. Some who have come were relatives of the people whose lives were saved by the courageous Ten Boom family. All the work there is done on a volunteer basis. No one, including the board of directors, of which I am chairman, has ever received any compensation for our work, and we have paid all our own expenses. A virtual tour of the museum is available at: http://www.tenboom.com/en/.

In 2002, I founded the Jerusalem Prayer Team (JPT) and

Churches United with Israel (CUWI). Then-mayor of Jerusalem, Ehud Olmert, flew to Dallas, Texas, to join me in launching JPT, an outreach of the Corrie ten Boom Fellowship.

As noted earlier, in 1844, a Ten Boom family patriarch had begun those weekly meetings to pray for the Jewish people, after a moving worship service in the Dutch Reformed Church of Reverend Witteveen. The first and second Great Awakenings that had swept Protestant Europe and North America played an important role in the yearning to pray for the Jewish people. Casper ten Boom felt the need to continue the weekly meetings, where his family and others who stopped by specifically prayed for the peace of Jerusalem (see Psalm 122:6). These meetings took place for one hundred years, until February 28, 1944, when Nazi soldiers raided the house and arrested members of the family for aiding local Jews. Following the tradition of the Ten Boom family, the Jerusalem Prayer Team was founded to encourage people to continue to pray for the peace of Jerusalem and to help the Jewish people—God's chosen ones.

In 2008, Casper and his daughter Betsie were posthumously honored at *Yad Vashem* as two of the Righteous Among the Nations. Corrie had been honored in 1968 and was knighted by the queen of the Netherlands for her work in helping save eight hundred men, women, and children during World War II. It was my great honor to have been invited to participate in the induction ceremony along with Israeli Ambassador to the Netherlands Harry Kney-Tal.

Through the years JPT has grown from that large rally in Dallas to several million people worldwide who receive weekly email updates. Churches United with Israel was formed to encourage churches to stand alongside the Jerusalem Prayer Team and encourage their members to actively pray for the Jewish people. It was the first organization of its kind and has some three hundred top church leaders on its board of governors.

Evangelicals are not engaged in terrorist attacks against their enemies; they are not intent upon doing God's work on earth *for* Him. They are, instead, advocates for the State of Israel; they are defenders of God's Word and His children. Many evangelical groups support programs to provide food, clothing, housing, and more for Jews who have returned to Israel, especially those from Russia. They employ whatever political clout has been amassed in order to stand in strong support of Israel. With millions of Christians in the world, their presence remains a force with which to be reckoned.

Those who support the Jewish people have expended billions of dollars in assistance to orphanages, and by providing medical supplies and sponsoring social-assistance programs for the poor and needy in Israel. Information is dispensed through conferences in support of the tiny nation, through promoting better understanding between Christians and Jews, by denouncing anti-Semitism, and through prayer. Various groups have sponsored marches through Jerusalem in support of the nation and the right of the Jewish people to live in Israel. Still others have aided Jews from Russia and other countries to immigrate to Israel. The Jerusalem Prayer Team has been at the forefront of these efforts to provide assistance to the Jewish people.

JPT has raised funds and invested millions of humanitarian dollars in Israel by providing food for the hungry, warm hats and coats for thousands of elderly Jews, basic necessities for Russian Jewish refugees, backpacks for schoolchildren, medical equipment for terror victims, and the reconstruction of a bomb shelter/community center in Jerusalem to be used as a safe place during terrorist strikes. It contains a kitchen, televisions, telephones, and much more. The Jerusalem Prayer Team helps to fund bomb shelters near schools for children to seek safety during rocket attacks. Our organization has also been asked to provide apartment buildings to house Holocaust survivors. It continues to invest in the lives and safety of the Jewish people in Israel, and prayers for Israel can be posted on an interactive prayer wall website open not only to JPT members but to people worldwide.

The stated purpose of the Jerusalem Prayer Team: to guard, defend, and protect the Jewish people and *Eretz Yisrael* until she is secure; to see Christians and Jews standing together to gain a better understanding of each other; to establish a strong and secure Bible Land; and to benevolently meet the needs of those whom Jesus describes in Matthew, chapter 25:

"For I was hungry and you gave Me food; I was thirsty and you gave Me drink; I was a stranger and you took Me in; I was naked and you clothed Me; I was sick and you visited Me; I was in prison and you came to Me. . . ."

And the King will answer and say to them, "Assuredly, I say to you, inasmuch as you did it to one of the least of these My brethren, you did it to Me."
—Matthew 25:35–36, 40

Perhaps the most important edict for Christians is to "pray for the peace of Jerusalem" (Psalm 122:6). God calls the land of Israel "My land" (Ezekiel 38:16) and ceded it to Israel by a blood covenant that is irrevocable. As we have seen, Christians are called to bless Israel. The chief way we can do that is through prayer. Nothing is more important than prayer, for God will do nothing without it. The fuel that moves the heart of God is prayer. God has a purpose and a prophetic plan for our nation and certainly for the nation of Israel, but it is dependent on our prayers. His will and His blessings are bound up in what we declare on this earth. His purposes and plans are more important than anything else we can do. Abraham was a striking example of the power of prayer.

Wherever Abraham pitched his tent and camped for a season with his household, he erected an altar of sacrifice and prayer. God heard Abraham's prayers, and He hears ours as we pray for the peace of Jerusalem.

Another focus is the dire threat Iran poses to Israel and the entire world, as its leaders strive to secure nuclear weapons. Evangelical Christian organizations are closing ranks to stand behind the nation of Israel during this time of danger. As I wrote in *Cursed*:

> Although no people group has been targeted more than the Jewish people, God has not allowed them to be exterminated. Many horrific attempts have been made to annihilate them, but such attempts have ended in utter failure, defeat, and humiliation for the perpetrators. From Pharaoh to Haman to Hitler, their efforts to destroy the Jewish people have ended ignominiously. Haman was hanged on the very gallows he had built for Queen Esther's uncle, Mordecai (Esther 7:10). Pharaoh "commanded all his people, saying, 'Every son who is born you shall cast into the river, and every daughter you shall save alive'" (Exodus 1:22). This ruler, who ordered every Hebrew male child to be thrown into the river, was drowned with his own army in the Red Sea!

In 2012, I traveled to Jerusalem to seek a location for a Christian Zionism Museum. Through the museum, my plan was that the accounts of Christians who played crucial roles in helping to promote, defend, support, and establish the modern State of Israel could be told, as well as the stories of those men and women who fulfilled the moral duty to rescue Jewish people from the Holocaust. I believed the museum should offer interactive displays, areas for research, and also provide a bond between those Christians who have aided Israel through the years. My vision was to have a place where their achievements could be shared with thousands of visitors yearly.

During that trip, I met the owners of a five-story edifice at 22 Yosef Rivlin Street, just a stone's throw from the Temple Mount. As Joshua circled Jericho, so I prayerfully circled the blocks around the area, seeking God's gracious approval to purchase the property. God granted me favor with the owners, for as we negotiated the price for the building, they not only lowered the price by $2 million but also carried the note interest-free to the end of 2014.

The Friends of Zion Heritage Center is now a reality and proudly stands in the heart of Jerusalem at 20 Yosef Rivlin Street in a prominent location overlooking Independence Park and within walking distance to the Old City. It is one more building block in the plan and purpose God has surely had for my life. The Friends of Zion Heritage Center (FOZ), a $100 million project gained ten million members just in its first year of operation. FOZ, just six hundred meters from the Temple Mount, is ground zero for the global Jerusalem Prayer Team prayer movement. With over one billion Christian Zionists worldwide, the goal is to unite them to stand with Israel and the Jewish people. FOZ now has a vast social network platform to mobilize Israel's greatest friends. The organization already has more than one million members in Indonesia alone, and is presently growing by the staggering rate of two million members monthly. A massive communication hub will soon be linked to the thousands of Christian television and radio outlets, as well as to churches and universities globally.

For decades, sympathetic Gentiles from around the world have joined Jewish people in the trenches. With each succeeding battle for existence, new Bible-believing Christians have sprung up to stand with the children of Israel in their struggle to survive. These are the men and women who are spotlighted in the new Museum of Christian Zionism in Jerusalem—those who have staunchly supported the Jewish people before, during, and after the formation of the State of Israel.

Today my heart is overflowing with gratitude to God, as the dream He placed in my spirit more than thirty years ago has become a reality. When the contract for the purchase of the building that houses the Friends of Zion Heritage was signed, I was reminded once again that every promise from God is certain and sure, no matter how long we have to wait for it.

Abraham waited for the promised birth of Isaac for some twenty-five years, but in God's perfect timing, the son of promise was born. When I first met with Prime Minister Menachem Begin more than thirty years ago and we agreed to work together to build a bridge between Christians and Jews, part of that dream was to have a permanent presence in the Holy City. Now we proudly point to this beautiful facility that ministers to the physical needs of the Jewish people and to the spiritual needs of Christians worldwide.

There is a God-given, biblical—and intimate—connection between Christians and Jews. Based on love and truth, and surrounded by prayer, it can never be broken. The Jewish Messiah and our Lord and Savior sprang from the root of Jesse and will occupy the throne of King David in Jerusalem, Mount Zion, when He returns.

19

I was glad when they said to me, "Let us go into the house of the Lord."
Our feet have been standing within your gates, O Jerusalem!
Jerusalem is built as a city that is compact together, where the tribes go up, the tribes of the Lord, to the Testimony of Israel, to give thanks to the name of the Lord.
For thrones are set there for judgment, the thrones of the house of David.
Pray for the peace of Jerusalem: "May they prosper who love you.
Peace be within your walls, prosperity within your palaces."
For the sake of my brethren and companions, I will now say, "Peace be within you."
Because of the house of the Lord our God I will seek your good.

—PSALM 122

Psalm 122 contains the simple directive, "Pray for the peace of Jerusalem," and for the majority of my adult life I've done just that. I've prayed for the peace and safety of that magnificent city, for its leadership, and for all who live there. My prayer has always been that God would lavish His favor upon her inhabitants, restrain the forces of evil that threaten to overwhelm them, and cause them to thrive even as they live in the midst of unprecedented challenges.

As I've grown in my understanding of what it means to be both Jewish and Christian, I've expanded my prayers to include that same supplication for Jews everywhere. It's been a fascinating effort, praying in a way that is informed by the knowledge of events affecting us all around the world.

In the churches where I speak and minister I've taught leaders about the importance of praying for Jerusalem, too. I've emphasized the necessity for us to come alongside the people of Israel, and Jerusalem in particular, to pray for their safety and well-being, and I've done my best to show pastors how to educate their congregations on this topic—to move beyond the typical questions of doctrine and polity to confront the actual, real-world issues that Jews in many nations face. I do that in every church, every conference, and every event both in the United States and abroad.

As my work with the people of Israel expanded, so did my ministry to the underground church in the Soviet Union grow through the 1970s and into the 1980s. I came to know an ever-widening circle of Christian leaders there, as well as a group of rabbis who lived in the areas where I visited. On each trip, I equipped the pastors with Bibles, gave them instruction, and helped educate their congregations. I also worked to put copies of the *Tanakh*—canonical Hebrew scripture—in the hands of Jewish leaders, many of whom were as much without their scripture in written form as were the churches and their members. To make that effort even more successful, I recruited leaders and members from the underground church to distribute copies of the *Tanakh* to their Jewish neighbors. No hidden agenda. No strings attached. Just one oppressed group trying to help another.

As part of that effort, I invited Christian leaders and church members from all over the Soviet Union to attend a gathering at the Olympic Convention Center in Moscow. They were more than somewhat concerned about meeting in public. Much of the time the people gathered in apartments, arriving alone or in pairs. Each came at different times so as to arouse as little suspicion as possible. I had prayed about it beforehand and the Lord assured me that this event would be held without causing anyone a problem. We notified the country's Christian leaders about the gathering, rented the hall, and located hotel rooms to accommodate those who wished to attend the meeting. We paid their travel costs and food expenses, too, and they came from various towns, cities, and small villages.

During that event we prayed for many things, but one morning I led the gathering in prayer for the Jews of Russia, many of whom came from families who had been oppressed for multiple generations. As I prayed, a verse from Isaiah exploded in my spirit. "I WILL SAY TO THE NORTH, 'GIVE THEM UP!'" (Isaiah 43:6).

Instantly I knew that God was on the move and as I prayed I heard Him say that He was going to release the Russian Jews in a modern-day fulfillment of that prophecy. I thought, *What a sight that would be—Jews moving to Israel in droves, and in fulfillment of prophecy.*

Later, I met privately with bishops and pastors from the underground church. I told them what I'd seen and heard while I prayed and asked them to enlist members of their congregations in an effort to take literature to the Jews living near them, literature that would instruct them to prepare for a modern-day exodus—a mass immigration of Jews from the Soviet Union to Israel. The bishops and pastors agreed and before long we began an amazing prophetic journey based on that single scripture that had been activated in my spirit. It was a voyage that saw tens of thousands of Jews released from the grasp of Soviet control and freed to make the journey to safety.

While we moved forward with the literature distribution efforts in the Soviet Union, the Holy Spirit said to me, "YOU MUST GO TO THE HOME OF CORRIE TEN BOOM AND PRAY. AS YOU PRAY, I WILL OPEN UP RUSSIA IN A MIGHTY WAY FOR YOU."

Going to Corrie ten Boom's family home seemed a rather strange path, but it would prove to be the very route that would lead me through Holland in order to help Russian Jews. Perhaps, not so strange after all, when I considered that Corrie and the entire Ten Boom family had been at the heart of the Jewish rescue effort during World War II. In obedience to the Holy Spirit, I flew to Holland and visited the Ten Boom home. By then, Corrie had gone on to her heavenly reward and we'd formed the Corrie ten Boom Fellowship, which purchased and restored the house. It has since operated as a museum and I've spent many hours there familiarizing myself with the house and meeting people who still remembered her.

During that particular trip, I spent a lot of time in prayer, listening for what God had to say about the things we were doing in Russia, and hoping not to miss the reason He'd sent me to Holland.

As I sat in the clock shop in prayer, there was a knock on the door. A woman named Erica van Eeghen entered and asked if she could see the Hiding Place—the room where Corrie and her family hid Jews while working fearlessly to get those in danger out of the city. I was glad to show her around, giving her a tour of the property. As she was leaving she handed me her card and invited me to join her and her husband for dinner that evening at their home.

Because she was a stranger, I would not normally have accepted her offer, but I found the Holy Spirit urging me, "THIS IS THE KEY TO THE SOVIET UNION." I accepted her invitation and later that evening a car arrived to take me to their home.

As we dined that evening in their beautiful abode outside Amsterdam, I learned that the woman who'd invited me was married to Ernst van Eeghen, a Dutch businessman who owned 114 corporations both in Holland and the Soviet Union. He held several Dutch consular titles and was a born-again Christian.

As I learned about this, I was overwhelmed. I had accepted the invitation to dine with them knowing nothing about their wealth or social status, or of their involvement in Russia. I'd come only out of obedience to the Lord, and the realization that He was using that moment to make possible the fulfillment of the Word He'd declared to me as I was praying that day in Moscow. Several times during the evening I found myself on the verge of tears.

Ernst noticed the look on my face as I strove to contain my emotions. "Is there something wrong with the food?"

"No. It's just that, while we were sitting here talking, the Holy Spirit revealed to me that you are going to be a major key to revival in Russia."

He looked over at his wife. "You told him?"

"No," she assured him. "I told him nothing."

As our conversation continued I learned that Van Eeghen had used his business influence in the Soviet Union to host several human rights conferences. Those gatherings, which came to be known as Berkenrode Consultations—a name derived from the title of the estate where the Van Eeghens lived—addressed a number of key issues affecting Soviet relations with the West. Along the way, Van Eeghen had become one of the most influential Westerners in the Soviet Union.

What Van Eeghen thought his wife had told me was almost exactly what I had said to him: "God told me," he explained, "that my ministry is to open up the Soviet Union for the gospel."

As we talked, he told me about a time when the head of the KGB had come to his house in great distress. "He said to me, 'I can't get the blood off my hands. I've scrubbed and scrubbed, but I can't get the blood of the innocent off my hands.'"

Ernst explained that only the blood of Jesus could cleanse his hands and then led the leader of the KGB to Christ. He showed me a letter he had received from the man filled with questions about the meaning of Scripture. The born-again KGB leader was used mightily as an instrument of God to help a number of ministries obtain permits to enter the Soviet Union. As I listened to the testimony of God's goodness, I thought of the lines from William Shakespeare's play "MacBeth," when the physician is summoned to attend a troubled and suicidal Lady MacBeth. The doctor's diagnosis? "More needs she the divine than the physician. God, God forgive us all!"

Through our conversation that night, Ernst van Eeghen became involved in our effort to bring as many Jews as possible from Russia to Israel. The underground church distributed literature telling Soviet Jews about the opportunities that awaited them in Israel and instructing them how to apply for travel documents. With the help of Van Eeghen's contacts at the Dutch Embassy, visas and passports were approved without a glitch. Together, we helped thousands find freedom and safety and watched while God fulfilled His word. Again I was reminded of the scripture in Isaiah 49:22:

> This is what the Sovereign Lord says: "See, I will give a signal to the godless nations. They will carry your little sons back to you in their arms; they will bring your daughters on their shoulders. (NLT)

Striving to help Russian Jews return to Israel was a highlight of our work in the Soviet Union, but it wasn't the end. In 1985, I felt prompted by God to produce a television special based on my book *Let My People Go*. One of the people highlighted in that production was the Russian dissident Natan Sharansky.

Sharansky was born to a Jewish family in Donetsk, a city in Ukraine. He was a child chess prodigy and graduated from the Moscow Institute of Physics and Technology with a degree in Applied Mathematics. After graduation, he applied for an exit visa to travel to Israel but was denied permission to leave the Soviet Union. Authorities supported their decision by asserting that he had been exposed to information that was vital to Soviet security and thus could not be permitted to travel outside the country.

After his exit visa was denied, Sharansky became involved in the protest movement, becoming a founding member of the Moscow Helsinki Group—one of the Refuseniks, a group of young Soviets who'd all been denied travel permission. In 1978, he was convicted of spying for the United States and sentenced to thirteen years in prison, a verdict that included solitary confinement and hard labor. He served time in several penal facilities.

Sharansky's wife, Avital, had been permitted to leave the Soviet Union, and while Natan was incarcerated she traveled throughout the West working to keep her husband's story and the plight of Soviet Jews always before the public. She lobbied leaders at every level of government to help gain his release and even published her own book, *Next Year in Jerusalem*, giving an account of their life and work among dissident Russian Jews.

I was well aware of their situation and wanted to help. My goal for the television project was to use it to acquire one million signatures on a petition calling for Sharansky's release. I intended to present that petition to President Reagan in an effort to enlist his help in freeing the Russian Jewish dissident. Reagan and Soviet leader Mikhail Gorbachev enjoyed a sometimes tense but eventually quite personable relationship. I thought that if Reagan pressed for Sharansky's release, Gorbachev might just free him and let him travel to Israel.

We created a script and sent crews all over the world to obtain taped footage for the show, then purchased television time to air it in every major market around the United States. Viewers responded enthusiastically and we accomplished our goal. I presented the petition with well over a million signatures to President Reagan and asked him to help. He agreed and, after intense negotiations, Sharansky was released.

When he arrived at the Ben Gurion Airport near Tel Aviv, Sharansky phoned President Reagan to thank him for his help. I was glad to have aided in this effort, though I wasn't the only one and certainly not the most important. Still, I know God had determined in His heart to set Sharansky free, and my participation was part of that.

After Soviet authorities began issuing exit visas for Jews to return to Israel, and after Sharansky had been released, I sensed the Holy Spirit telling me that I would preach in the Kremlin Palace. I was astounded by what I heard but certain the voice I heard in my spirit was indeed the voice of the Lord. That revelation again drove me to my knees in prayer where I figuratively drew a circle of prayer around the Soviet Union.

The Moscow Kremlin is a vast complex that includes five palaces, four cathedrals, and many other buildings, the most recent addition a helipad authorized by President Vladimir Putin. The Kremlin sits atop Borovitsky Hill, a strategic location that has been occupied since the eleventh century and has been the seat of power, more or less, since that time. Today, the Grand Kremlin Palace, the largest building in the complex, is the official residence of the Russian Federation president. However, it is little used as a residence and its five reception halls are rented out for special events. I intended to hold an event in one of those halls.

In addition to having many historic buildings, the Kremlin has come to be the home of the Russian government. During the Soviet era, it was the site where Communist leaders cursed God and vowed to bury America. It is the site from which various leaders issued edicts and decrees that resulted in the persecution of Jews, the church, and imposed limitations on personal freedom suffered by many, including Natan Sharansky and the Refuseniks.

In obedience to what I'd heard from the Holy Spirit, I flew to Moscow and applied for permission to hold a meeting in one of the Kremlin Palace's reception halls. I was turned down seventeen times, but on the eighteenth time, permission was granted.

We advertised the event as an Easter musical, hired an orchestra, and located a ballet company that was interested in performing. As a way of saying thank you to the underground church, I invited the members to attend and made sure a place was available for those who came.

On the night of the event, every seat in the palace hall was filled. The orchestra played magnificently. The dancers performed beautifully, and then I preached. It was Easter, God had said I would speak to the crowd, so I preached. As I spoke that evening I said, "Stalin is dead. Lenin is dead. But Jesus Christ is alive."

You can imagine, those words did not sit well with the palace guards. When I continued, they attempted to remove me from the stage. They quickly saw that would produce a major incident so they cut the electrical power to the microphone and turned out the lights in the room where we met.

Inspired by the Holy Spirit, I shouted, "Those who have shut off the lights and microphone do not respect your president! I was about to pray for him." Seconds later, power was restored to the microphone and lights in the room came back on.

It was a marvelous evening—as Easter should be. Not only did God permit me to proclaim the gospel in the Grand Kremlin Palace, He also arranged to have it aired on Moscow's Channel One, at that time the largest network in Russia. Its viewership included more than 125 million people in eleven time zones, which also made it one of the largest networks in the world. We aired the event live during prime time that evening, and then rebroadcast it a few days later. That was the first time anyone had ever proclaimed the gospel in the Grand Kremlin Palace, held an altar call, and had it aired live over Russian television. God certainly does the impossible!

What I could not know when I had earlier knelt in prayer was that God would make a way for me to speak to the Russian people; that before I called, He had answered just as He had promised in Isaiah 65:24. God always operates in future tense. Romans 4:17b reminds us that "God, who gives life to the dead . . . calls those things which do not exist as though they did."

Author Mark Batterson reminds us:

> God cannot be bribed or blackmailed. God doesn't do miracles to satisfy our selfish whims. God does miracles for one reason and one reason alone: to spell His glory. We just happen to be the beneficiaries.

20

*"Whereas you have been forsaken and hated,
so that no one went through you,
I will make you an eternal excellence, a joy of many generations."*

—ISAIAH 60:15

One year, Carolyn and I invited my father to Texas for Thanksgiving, but I strongly felt we couldn't have him at the house. As it turned out, circumstances were such that we had to postpone his visit.

I phoned Dad to explain the situation to him and, as I expected, he didn't take it well. Just as it was when I was a child, he screamed and ranted, calling me a liar and a phony. "You moron," he chided. "Now what am I supposed to do? You screwed up my Thanksgiving!" I let him say whatever he wanted but held firm on my resolve that he couldn't come to the house, and the call ended as badly as it had begun.

For a week after that, I endured the "slings and arrows of outrageous fortune" flung at me by the consummate liar, Satan himself;

and then I got angry. That's when I circled the prayer wagons and began to pray about my father's surly response. God's answer was not at all what I expected. Rather than a spiritual pat on the back and a customary gold star for good behavior, the Holy Spirit instructed me to seek my father's forgiveness. Instead of pouting about God's response, I immediately made travel arrangements to meet with my dad. Once I was face-to-face with him I said, "Dad, God told me to get on my knees, humble myself in your presence, and apologize to you."

Before he could respond, I dropped to the floor beside his chair and began to confess my failures as a son—pride, failing to pray for him and often refusing to do so, and many other things. I didn't enumerate his wrongs against me. Nor did I relive either the beatings I had suffered at his hands or the curses I had received from his mouth. I simply confessed the sins I knew I'd committed.

Then I began to talk to him about salvation, and as I did, a horrified look came over his face. "Stop," he demanded. "I've heard enough. I can't take any more. I can never be saved. My home will be eternal hell."

Undeterred by his response, I talked to Dad about Jesus and what He meant in my life, the changes He'd brought in me, and the work yet to be done. As I spoke, his hard exterior began to crack and he opened up to me in ways he'd never done before. He told me of his childhood, the abuse he'd received from his father, and how he had been made to work in the fields from the time he was five or six years old. Then he leaned forward in his seat and gripped my hands so hard his knuckles turned white. "Son," he sobbed, "I should have been put in prison for what I done to you."

Tears ran down his face, and in that moment God's grace and mercy filled me with genuine compassion for the man I thought I could never forgive, much less love. I led him to Christ that afternoon.

Later, as I thought about God's answer to my prayers, I was reminded of a scripture He'd given me years before. As with many others, this one was from Isaiah:

> Arise, shine; for your light has come! And the glory of the LORD is risen upon you. For behold, the darkness shall cover the earth, and deep darkness the people; but the LORD will arise over you, and His glory will be seen upon you. The Gentiles shall come to your light, and kings to the brightness of your rising. Lift up your eyes all around, and see: They all gather together, they come to you; your sons shall come from afar, and your daughters shall be nursed at your side. —Isaiah 60:1–4

Having reminded me again of that passage, I knew God would honor it in my life, but like many other scriptures He'd given me, this one was quite general in its application. It could apply in a broad context. I needed to know what He meant on a more practical level, and so I asked. The response I received was astounding and incisive.

As clearly as I've ever heard Him, the Holy Spirit said, "GO TO SAUDI ARABIA, DEFEND ISRAEL, AND PREACH MY WORD."

That was a total "wow" moment! Go to Saudi Arabia? I'm Jewish. Saudis are Arabs, and not just Arabs but Muslims, and not merely Muslim but Wahhabi, one of the strictest, most orthodox of all Sunni Muslim groups.

"I can't go to Saudi Arabia," I argued. "Billy Graham hasn't even been there. And I'm Jewish. They cut off the heads of Jews in Saudi Arabia."

The Lord replied, "BILLY NEVER APPLIED FOR A VISA. APPLY."

I drove down to a visa processing service and applied for a visa to Saudi Arabia—never for a moment thinking my request would be approved. One week later the visa arrived at the place where I had initially applied.

After all that had happened in my life, one might expect that I would have realized God was at work and, after having come to that realization, that I would repent of my attitude, align my actions with God's actions, and rejoice. No! Instead, I continued to argue with the Creator of the universe.

"Okay," I said. "I have a visa. But I have no invitation to speak. No meetings scheduled. No other reason to go. I don't even know a single person who lives there. How do You expect me to do this?"

In response to all of that, God was surprisingly silent and in that silence all I heard was the memory of His voice when He told me to go. That's when I knew beyond question that I had no choice but to obey.

With visa in hand, I quickly made flight arrangements, and just two weeks later climbed aboard a British Airways flight for Saudi Arabia. Twenty long, exhausting hours later, it landed in Dhahran, a Saudi Arabian city on the Persian Gulf. I was exhausted.

After clearing customs I took a taxi to the Gulf Meridian Hotel in Al Khobar, checked in to a room, and collapsed on the bed. "Father," I prayed. "Here I am. Now what?"

When I looked around, I saw a Saudi telephone book lying on the nightstand beside the bed. I opened it and randomly flipped through the pages. I can't read a word of Arabic, but the book fell open to a page with an advertisement for the Dhahran Hotel. The advertisement was written in English. And once more God said, "Go."

Suddenly energized, I ran into the bathroom, splashed cold water on my face, and combed my hair. Then I re-tucked my shirt, straightened my jacket, and raced downstairs to the concierge. Minutes later, I was seated in a taxi for the ride to the Dhahran Hotel.

As we arrived at the lobby entrance, I saw a banner draped across the front of the hotel that read "Joint Operation Command." I grinned from ear to ear. The hotel was headquarters for US forces being assembled to liberate Kuwait from Saddam Hussein and his Republican Guard. The army's effort was still part of Desert Shield. The Gulf War—code named Desert Storm—was still months away.

In addition to housing the Army Command, the hotel also was headquarters for television networks that were covering the war.

Without a moment's hesitation, I climbed from the taxi, tucked my Bible under my arm, and started through the hotel lobby entrance.

Americans were everywhere. I stopped the first official-looking person I met, stuck out my hand, and said, "How are you?"

The man looked at me in horror and asked in English, "Who are you? And what on earth are you doing with that Bible?"

"I'm Mike Evans," I replied. "I'm from the United States."

"You can't be," he muttered in a tone of disbelief.

"But I am."

"Then you're going to jail."

I frowned. "Why? I just got here."

"Christian ministers are not allowed into the country. How did you get here?"

"British Airlines," I smiled. "They have flights in here three times a week."

His tone changed and his demeanor became all business. "Go back to your hotel," he directed. "Pack your belongings. And be out of here within forty-eight hours. If you aren't gone by then, you *will* go to jail."

He seemed so certain, I began to think maybe he was right—maybe I would go to jail. Perhaps God's will for me was to preach in prison as had the apostle Paul. Or maybe I was mistaken in what I thought I was supposed to do. Maybe I wasn't supposed to be there at all. Or maybe just not at that hotel. As I pondered what I believed to be my Holy Spirit–directed assignment, a story came to mind:

> As a minister was addressing a group of men, he

took a large piece of paper and made a black dot in the center of it with a marking pen. Then he held the paper up before the group and asked them what they saw. One person quickly replied, "I see a black mark." "Right," the preacher replied. "What else do you see?" Complete silence prevailed. "Don't you see anything other than the dot?" he asked. A chorus of noes came from the audience. "I'm really surprised," the speaker commented. "You have completely overlooked the most important thing of all—the sheet of paper." Then he made the application. He said that in life we are often distracted by small, dot-like disappointments or painful experiences, and we are prone to forget the innumerable blessings we receive from the hand of the Lord. But like the sheet of paper, the good things are far more important than the adversities that monopolize our attention.

Perplexed by what the man said, and with no other plan to follow, I made my way back to the hotel lobby and stepped outside determined to focus on the "bigger things." A few minutes later, a taxi arrived and I climbed into the back seat. I gave the driver directions back to my hotel and began to pray.

En route, we passed in front of a gate at the headquarters compound for the Eighty-Second Airborne—the army unit my friend Jim and I had wanted to join when we had enlisted as teenagers almost thirty years earlier. I ordered the driver to stop and got out, paid for the ride and then walked over to the gate. A guard stepped out to meet me.

"I need to speak to the chaplain," I told the guard.

"Who are you?"

"I'm Mike Evans from Dallas, Texas."

The guard looked as puzzled as the man at the hotel. "How did you get here?"

"British Airways," I again replied. If they could ask silly questions, I could respond with silly answers.

"You, sir, will go to jail."

"I've already been told that. Now, may I please speak to the chaplain?"

A flurry of phone calls followed, and eventually the guard let me enter, then directed me to the proper office. The chaplain, however, gave me the same response as everyone else. "I don't know how in the world you were allowed into the country. What do you want?"

Later I learned that chaplains assigned to the US military in Muslim countries are not allowed to wear crosses on their uniforms; nor do they walk around with a Bible tucked under their arm. In fact, they aren't even called chaplains. Instead, they go by titles such as "Recreational and Motivational Coordinator." Obviously, I didn't know that when I first arrived; I just knew God told me to go to Saudi Arabia. So in response to the chaplain's question I said, "I want to speak to the troops."

He shook his head in wonder before answering: "Well, I'll call them together for you and then I'm leaving."

From that day until the day I flew back to Texas, I was privileged to preach to our troops stationed in Saudi Arabia. It was both humbling and encouraging to know that God was using me to minister to men and women serving so far from home and in such precarious circumstances.

One day, while riding through the streets of Dhahran, I noticed a group of soldiers gathered on a street corner. I stopped the cab, paid the fare, and climbed out. Though I'd been warned many times about openly sharing the gospel, I walked over to the group, turned to a passage of Scripture, and began to preach.

From behind me I heard a beautiful baritone voice singing "His Eye Is on the Sparrow." I turned to see an army sergeant from the United States and stopped what I was doing to listen. Tears streamed down my face as he sang the old hymn written in 1905, yet still timeless:

> When Jesus is my portion
> My constant friend is he
> His eye is on the sparrow
> And I know he watches me
> His eye is on the sparrow
> And I know he watches me

Soon the other men joined him. At the conclusion of the song, they began to share testimonies of God's grace and protection. It was a magnificent display of God's presence, and several of the men that day gave their lives to Christ.

As we talked and prayed together, a military policeman walked up. He pushed his way into the center of our gathering and glanced warily in my direction. "What are you doing? It's against the law to preach in public. We can take you to jail."

"That's fine," I said. "Do whatever you have to do. Everyone tells me I'm going there anyway." The officer wasn't amused but he didn't arrest me, either.

When I returned to my hotel that evening, I wanted nothing more than a shower to wash away the dust and grime of the sand-covered streets. I was hot and tired, and my bed with cool, clean sheets was calling my name.

As I walked through the lobby, though, I was told members of the Kuwaiti royal family were gathered in one of the lounges. When the Iraqi army invaded, they had been driven out of Kuwait. Most of them had taken up residence in Saudi Arabia. Their presence in the lounge surprised me but I was further stunned when one of the young men from their gathering left the others and hurried in my direction.

"I know you." He grinned as he reached me. "You're a friend of Yasser Arafat. I saw you with him in Geneva."

The irony of the situation was not lost on me. True, I had been with Arafat in Geneva, but he and I were not at all on friendly terms. I was about to laugh at the young man's remark when the Holy Spirit nudged me. Rather than refuting his assertion, I found myself saying, "You will soon be going home. This war will be short and with little bloodshed. You will regain your country and when you do, you must give the glory to Jesus."

"Are you a prophet?"

"No, I am not. But this is a word to you from God."

The young man stepped back and looked at me intently. "If this prophecy comes to pass, you shall be a guest of the royal family in Kuwait." I smiled, shook his hand, and continued on my way toward the elevator.

That night as I lay in bed thinking about the events of the day and about the young man I'd seen in the lobby, the Enemy once again attacked me. *"You are going to jail. You are doomed. They will hide you away in there and you'll never get out. You had better just pack up and go home now."*

As I prayed and rebuked Satan, the Holy Spirit spoke to me. "RETURN TO THE DHAHRAN HOTEL. SPEAK TO THE FIRST PERSON YOU SEE AND ASK IF YOU CAN GO WITH HIM."

Early the next morning I took a taxi back to the hotel and entered the lobby. As I entered, a man was coming toward me. He was an Arab, about six feet tall, with short black hair and dressed in a Saudi Arabian military uniform. From the insignia I could see that he was a four-star general.

As the Lord had instructed me, I stuck out my hand and said, "Can I go with you?"

The man shook my hand and stared at me with a puzzled expression. When he didn't respond, I repeated my question. "May I go with you?"

"What is your name?"

"Mike Evans."

"And you are from where?"

"The United States of America."

His demeanor changed. "Be here tomorrow at 0600 and you shall go with me."

The next morning I stood outside the hotel at 0545. At precisely 0600 a dozen vehicles drove up and in the fourth jeep was a four-star general, Prince Khalid, the man whose hand I had shaken the day before. I was waved inside and sat down beside the general.

As the jeep started forward, General Khalid glanced down at my lap. A Bible rested there and he looked up at me with raised eyebrows. "Are you a Christian?"

"Yes, I am—and a minister."

"We behead ministers in the square every Thursday. Would you like to go *there* with me, too?"

"I'm busy Thursday," I answered.

A grin broke over General Khalid's face. "I like you."

We soon reached an airfield where the general, his retinue, and I traveled by helicopter to the Kuwait border where he met with Syrian High Command and the leaders of the Egyptian Third Army. I listened while they briefed Khalid on their invasion operations.

When the briefing concluded, Khalid asked me to accompany him as he inspected the troops. I had no idea what I was supposed to do and turned to one of the men in the entourage. "What do I do?"

Because I was an American, the man thought I was from the Defense Department and assigned to General Khalid in an official capacity. He also thought I was aware of his own assignment and therefore kept no secrets from me. From him I learned details about Operation Bright Star, a joint US–Egyptian exercise that would take on added significance with the approaching 1991 Gulf War.

Later that day we joined the military leaders for lunch. After Prince Khalid introduced me, he surprisingly became my interpreter when I was able to share a short presentation of the gospel with the soldiers. He surely had not expected that turn of events when he invited me along.

After lunch, Prince Khalid asked me what was next on my agenda and I replied that I wanted to speak to the troops in the field. He called in a French Foreign Legion helicopter to take me to minister to the men and women who had dug in on the front line.

Several years after that trip to the Persian Gulf and my meeting with Prince Khalid, I preached a crusade in the Philippines. A trio of Filipino pastors greeted me warmly after the meeting and one even began to cry. I thought I hadn't preached well enough to bring tears to anyone's eyes, so I asked why he was crying. Shocked that I didn't know, one of the other men told me they had been in jail in

Dhahran—condemned to be beheaded for preaching the gospel. One day without any fanfare, their cell doors were opened and they were told they could leave. It seems that a general also known as Prince Khalid had arranged for their freedom. The Filipino pastor was weeping because he knew what I'd never known—that my witness to Prince Khalid had saved their lives.

21

*It is the Lord your God you must follow,
and him you must revere.
Keep his commands and obey him;
serve him and hold fast to him.*

—Deuteronomy 13:4 NIV

After the terrorist attacks of September 11, 2001, the United States declared war against that group of terrorists in Afghanistan known as Al-Qaeda and its sponsor, a quasi-Islamic government known as the Taliban. Two years later, the United States invaded Iraq as part of a global war against terror. As US troops advanced across Iraq, the Holy Spirit prompted me to write a book on the war and what could happen once it ended.

As is often my practice when presented with a challenge, I first circled this instruction from God with prayer, and then I opened my Bible and began to read. The scripture that leapt from the pages was from Psalm 1:1–3 (NIV):

> Blessed is the one who does not walk in step with the wicked or stand in the way that sinners take or sit in the company of mockers, but whose delight is in the law of the Lord, and who meditates on his law day and night.
>
> That person is like a tree planted by streams of water, which yields its fruit in season and whose leaf does not wither—whatever they do prospers.

This was the same scripture God had given me years earlier, after I had returned from Korea and lived at the YMCA in Philadelphia. He reminded me of it again in 1979, when He prompted me to write my first book, *Israel: America's Key to Survival*. The manuscript for that book turned out well and I thought it would make a great documentary, but no traditional publisher would publish it, and no producer would make a movie about it. So, after eighteen rejection slips from publishing houses, I self-published the book. I also produced a documentary, all the while trusting God that whatever I did, He would prosper. That book sold more than fifty thousand copies the first week it was released.

This time, the book the Holy Spirit impressed me to write would be entitled *Beyond Iraq: The Next Move—Ancient Prophecy and Modern Day Conspiracy Collide*. Hoping it might become a *New York Times* best seller, I went to work on it the moment I thought of it, vanishing into my study for nineteen hours a day. A few days later, the first draft of the book was completed.

When the book was released, I received another scripture from the Lord; this one from Joshua: "No man shall be able to stand before you all the days of your life; as I was with Moses, so I will be with you. I will not leave you nor forsake you" (Joshua 1:5).

Energized by that verse, my staff placed phone calls to all the major networks in New York City, seeking an opportunity for me to appear on various news shows to discuss the book. After hours of hard work, one commitment from a single program airing on a Christian network was secured. It was only one show, but I was overjoyed to have that opening; sadly, the show's producer called to cancel my appearance.

The news was disappointing, but rather than wallow in it I left my study, went to my prayer room, and fell on my knees before God. I reminded Him that I wrote the book at His prompting. That it was His idea and I had done my best to be obedient in producing it. Now I needed Him to intervene once more and help us publicize the book.

As I lay on the floor before God, circling my writing endeavor with prayer, the Word from those verses in Psalm 1:3 flooded my mind and I heard the Lord say, "WHATEVER YOU DO WILL PROSPER." With those words resounding in my spirit, I knew what to do. I would travel to New York City and call on every news personality at every major network.

That was a big job, so I left the prayer room, called my daughter Rachel, and asked if she would accompany me. She readily agreed to help, and the next morning we boarded a flight from Dallas.

When we reached our hotel in New York I said to Rachel, "If Jesus doesn't make this publicity effort a success, we will have failed completely. But I'd rather fail knowing I had faith in the Lord than in the flesh."

The next morning, we each took a stack of books and made the rounds of the television studios, handing out copies and asking for interviews. Afterward, we returned to my room and waited for the phone to ring. Nothing happened.

On Sunday, Rachel and I attended Times Square Church, pastored by my old friend and Teen Challenge founder Rev. David Wilkerson. After the service, he prayed with me about the launch of the book and its success. I appreciated his prayer, but as we left the church I was uncertain whether we should stay in New York or return to Texas the following day. Rachel and I talked about it on the way back to our room and by the time we arrived, it seemed that the Holy Spirit was urging me to stay in the city one more night.

The next morning, as we prepared to leave for home, my cell phone rang. The caller was a producer for Neil Cavuto from the Fox News network; he asked if I would appear for an interview on the network. We were delighted for the opportunity, but that was only the beginning. Over the next several months, I was invited to promote the book on sixty-one television and radio programs. By June of that year, *Beyond Iraq* had sold 53,000 copies. In July, it hit the *New York Times,* one of a long list of books on its best-seller list, reaching as high as the top ten. God had given me great favor. The verse in 1 Samuel 15:22 sprang to mind, "Behold, to obey is better than sacrifice."

That book marked the beginning of a writing career for me. In 2003 alone, I released three titles—*God Wrestling*; *The Unanswered Prayers of Jesus*; and *The Prayer of David*. A steady stream of books followed as God blessed me with favor in an unusual way.

That is precisely how God works. As Joseph told his brothers in Genesis 50:20, "But as for you, you meant evil against me; but God meant it for good, in order to bring it about as it is this day, to save many people alive."

Satan meant for me to fail in the pursuit of obedience. Jehovah took that plan for evil and turned it into good in ways I could not have seen. Pastor and author Max Lucado writes:

> God, the Master Weaver. He stretches the yarn and intertwines the colors, the ragged twine with the velvet strings, the pains with the pleasures. Nothing escapes his reach. Every king, despot, weather pattern, and molecule are at his command. He passes the shuttle back and forth across the generations, and as He does, a design emerges. Satan weaves; God reweaves.

Have you ever known a Christian who worked diligently and enjoyed success beyond measure? Who seemed to lead a charmed life, finding favor with both God and man? My friend, luck has nothing to do with such success. If you look more closely, you will likely find that the person in question is a tireless and dedicated servant of God, a prayer warrior who seeks God's will at every turn. Missionary John Hyde discovered the key to powerful prayer:

> We need to be still before Him, so as to hear His voice and allow Him to pray in us—nay, allow Him to pour into our souls His overflowing life of intercession, which means literally: face to face meeting with God—real union and communion.

Does it mean that the prayer warrior has never faced challenges or hard times? Not at all; it simply means that through the good times and bad, he or she has faithfully served God with the confidence that a loving heavenly Father would grant them favor with both Him and man and turn every problem into an opportunity for blessing.

When God grants favor with man, it can accomplish what personality, ability, talent, and exertion may not achieve. Such favor can miraculously open doors that might normally remain tightly closed and locked. It can create opportunities otherwise unavailable.

One of the great buzzwords of the millennial generation is *networking*. It is a means to further one's career path, to meet people with like interests. God's favor is networking at its very highest and best. So don't hesitate to pray for God's favor; but while you pray, walk uprightly before Him and extend grace and favor to those you meet along the way. Psalm 84:11 says, "For the Lord God is a sun and shield; the Lord will give grace and glory; no good thing will He withhold from those who walk uprightly." And that includes favor with man.

AFTERWORD

The Lord has heard my supplication;
the Lord will receive my prayer.

—PSALM 6:9

You and I cannot make contact with God without prayer. If we don't make that connection, no matter how sincere our intentions, we will not see a change in the circumstances of our life. Pastor and author Dr. Charles Stanley wrote of prayer:

> I would say to anybody: the greatest lesson you can learn is to learn to live by faith on your face before God. You can face anything, no matter what it is. He said, "I'll never leave you or forsake you," but if I'm so busy I'm not listening to him, I'm not waiting for him, I'm not expecting him to do something—I think people face a lot of circumstances and go through a lot of heartache and trouble that would be unnecessary if they would just stop and listen.

Often, I think we are like little children—not so much hard of hearing as we are hard of *listening*. We hear, but we do not necessarily heed His warnings. Learning to hear God's voice from scripture—learning the way He expressed Himself to the men and women of old—teaches us how to distinguish the sound of His voice from our own and helps us avoid the deceptive whispers of the Enemy.

My journey to wholeness in Christ has been painful at times, but it is not an unfamiliar path. I meet people all the time who feel that in order to get God's attention they must do more, work harder, talk louder, be smarter, but God tells us that in order to hear Him we must wait and seek and listen closely. Seeking first the Kingdom and His righteousness leads us to increased faith and less worry. Peace and worry cannot occupy the same space. One forces the other out. Instead of doing more, we must learn to worship at His feet. Our prayer should be, "Help me to wait patiently for the very best You have for my life."

God places watchmen on the walls of our lives. I call them Esthers and Nehemiahs . . . people such as Corrie ten Boom and, perhaps, people like you. The world has figuratively been scratching its collective head trying to find an answer to the ongoing crisis in the Bible land. That answer is in your hands and mine—we just have to hear from God, through prayer and intercession.

Abraham is a striking example of the power of prayer. He interceded for Sodom and for his nephew Lot's sake, and God delayed judgment. God would have spared Sodom for ten righteous souls (Genesis

18:20–33). Abraham thought surely Lot and his wife, their daughters, their sons, and their sons-in-law would be righteous and number more than ten. Unfortunately, he was wrong. Not every member of Lot's family was righteous. Even his daughters and wife had to be led from the city under protest. Mrs. Lot was so upset that she turned to look at all she was forced to leave behind and suffered Jehovah's judgment when she was turned into a pillar of salt. Abraham's pleas were to no avail because of Lot's choices. Sodom was destroyed.

Abraham was an intercessor. Wherever he pitched his tent and camped with his household for a season, he erected an altar of sacrifice and prayer. Even when he got into big trouble by falsely telling King Abimelech that his wife, Sarah, was his sister, God honored Abraham's prayers. Abimelech realized he had taken another man's wife, and God said to Abimelech, "Now therefore, restore the man's wife; for he is a prophet, and he will pray for you and you shall live" (Genesis 20:7). God heard Abraham's prayers, and He hears ours. He wants us to be part of His dream and His team.

One of the great prayers of intercession in the Scriptures is recorded in Numbers 14:11–20. The Hebrew charges that had been placed in Moses' care were testing the patience of their leader and Jehovah. The continual complaining was wearing very thin:

> The LORD said to Moses, "How long will these people treat me with contempt? How long will they refuse to believe in me, in spite of all the signs I have performed

among them? I will strike them down with a plague and destroy them, but I will make you into a nation greater and stronger than they." Moses said to the Lord, "Then the Egyptians will hear about it! By your power you brought these people up from among them. And they will tell the inhabitants of this land about it. They have already heard that you, Lord, are with these people and that you, Lord, have been seen face to face, that your cloud stays over them, and that you go before them in a pillar of cloud by day and a pillar of fire by night. If you put all these people to death, leaving none alive, the nations who have heard this report about you will say, 'The Lord was not able to bring these people into the land he promised them on oath, so he slaughtered them in the wilderness.' "Now may the Lord's strength be displayed, just as you have declared: 'The Lord is slow to anger, abounding in love and forgiving sin and rebellion. Yet he does not leave the guilty unpunished; he punishes the children for the sin of the parents to the third and fourth generation.' In accordance with your great love, forgive the sin of these people, just as you have pardoned them from the time they left Egypt until now." The Lord replied, "I have forgiven them, as you asked." (NIV)

In Mark, chapter 9, the disciples came to Jesus, frustrated and downcast. A father had brought his child to them for healing. The little boy had what his father described as a "dumb spirit." After Jesus rebuked the spirit and the little boy was healed, the disciples privately asked Him why *they* could not heal the child. Jesus answered, "This kind can come out by nothing but prayer and fasting" (Mark 9:29).

September 11, 2001, was an assault from hell, planned and executed by demon spirits, just as have been other attacks worldwide—Paris, London, San Diego, Boston, Las Vegas, New York. The continuing terrorist attacks in Israel, and indeed worldwide, are a result of the same dark spiritual powers. These powers cannot be defeated without prayer. Praying saints are God's agents to carry out His will on Earth. Israel, the United States, and all other nations are helpless without prayer. If Jesus said that He could do nothing without prayer, then we surely cannot hope to accomplish anything of eternal value and significance without prayer. It was President Abraham Lincoln who said:

> I have been driven many times upon my knees by the overwhelming conviction that I had nowhere else to go. My own wisdom and that of all about me seemed insufficient for that day.

A Christian who refuses to pray is like a swimmer who refuses to enter the water. All the talk in the world about swimming will only bring skepticism and laughter if he never dives in and begins to swim. For a Christian to refuse to make prayer his or her number one priority is like saying to the world's vilest dictator, "We have laid down our weapons of warfare. You win!"

Our weapons of war and our Commander in Chief are waiting to win the battle; we only need to speak the Word. God has given us the weapons we need to successfully war against the enemy of our souls (Ephesians 6:13–17), the means to become effective intercessors:

> Therefore take up the whole armor of God, that you may be able to withstand in the evil day, and having done all, to stand. Stand therefore, having girded your waist with truth, having put on the breastplate of righteousness, and having shod your feet with the preparation of the gospel of peace; above all, taking the shield of faith with which you will be able to quench all the fiery darts of the wicked one. And take the helmet of salvation, and the sword of the Spirit, which is the word of God.

The Word of God in Isaiah 59:16 tells us of one of the purposes of God in sending His Son to die for you and me:

> He saw that there was no man, and wondered that there was no intercessor . . .

Just as the high priest was the go-between for the children of Israel and Jehovah, so we read in Hebrews 7:24–27:

> But He, because He continues forever, has an unchangeable priesthood. Therefore He is also able to save to the uttermost those who come to God through Him, since He always lives to make intercession for them. For such a High Priest was fitting for us, who is holy, harmless, undefiled, separate from sinners, and has become higher than the heavens; who does not need daily, as those high priests, to offer up sacrifices, first for His own sins and then for the people's, for this He did once for all when He offered up Himself.

If you wish to find a pattern for an intercessor, look no further than our Lord. Read His prayer in John 17. He prayed for the sick, the dispossessed, the lost, the wounded, and the downtrodden. He continues His intercession even today.

Jesus has provided tools for us to touch heaven in intercessory prayer. In Ephesians 6:18, Paul records why we need to use those gifts: "praying always with all prayer and supplication in the Spirit." Prayer is not for the faint of heart; it is hard work! As Scottish author and theologian Oswald Chambers wrote:

> We tend to use prayer as a last resort, but God wants it to be our first line of defense. We pray when there's nothing else we can do, but God wants us to pray before we do anything at all.
>
> Most of us would prefer, however, to spend our

time doing something that will get immediate results. We don't want to wait for God to resolve matters in His good time because His idea of 'good time' is seldom in sync with ours.

My life has been bathed in prayer, protected by prayer, and guided by prayer. I have asked, sought, and knocked according to Matthew 7:7, "Ask, and it will be given to you; seek, and you will find; knock, and it will be opened to you."

John Hyde, the nineteenth-century missionary known as "the apostle of prayer," wrote of that particular verse:

> Observe the progress in intensified desire—great, greater, greatest, and the corresponding reward till, to crown it all, the Father's heart is thrown open to us.

Blind English preacher William Walford wrote what may be the consummate hymn about prayer:

> Sweet hour of prayer! sweet hour of prayer!
> That calls me from a world of care,
> And bids me at my Father's throne
> Make all my wants and wishes known.
> In seasons of distress and grief,
> My soul has often found relief,
> And oft escaped the tempter's snare,
> By thy return, sweet hour of prayer!

SCRIPTURES ON PRAYER
—*from the*—
KING JAMES VERSION

Jeremiah 33:3—Call unto me, and I will answer thee, and shew thee great and mighty things, which thou knowest not.

Psalm 34:17—The righteous cry, and the LORD heareth, and delivereth them out of all their troubles.

Matthew 26:41—Watch and pray, that ye enter not into temptation: the spirit indeed is willing, but the flesh is weak.

Mark 11:24—Therefore I say unto you, What things soever ye desire, when ye pray, believe that ye receive them, and ye shall have them.

Luke 18:1—And he spake a parable unto them to this end, that men ought always to pray, and not to faint;

John 15:7—If ye abide in me, and my words abide in you, ye shall ask what ye will, and it shall be done unto you.

Ephesians 6:18—Praying always with all prayer and supplication in the Spirit, and watching thereunto with all perseverance and supplication for all saints;

Philippians 4:6—Be careful for nothing; but in every thing by prayer and supplication with thanksgiving let your requests be made known unto God.

1 Thessalonians 5:17—Pray without ceasing.

1 Timothy 2:5—For there is one God, and one mediator between God and men, the man Christ Jesus;

James 5:16—Confess your faults one to another, and pray one for another, that ye may be healed. The effectual fervent prayer of a righteous man availeth much.

Endnotes

1. Writer: David Phelps, Copyright: Winkin Music, Soulwriter Music Co. Inc., http://www.songlyrics.com/david-phelps/end-of-the-beginning-lyrics/#3zwiBvW6dRwwQoXq.99; accessed August 2015.

2. Dr. Paul Chappell, "Prayer is not..." Sunday, May 2, 2010, http://www.dailyintheword.org/content/prayer-not; accessed November 2017.

3. "What does it mean to pray without ceasing?" Got Questions Ministries, https://www.gotquestions.org/pray-without-ceasing.html; accessed October 2017.

4. Paul Lee Tan, *Encyclopedia of 7,700 Illustrations: Signs of the Times*, "Prayer Costs," 4586 (Rockville, MD: Assurance Publishers), 1052.

5. Dr. Noreen Jacks, "The Stigma of Infertility in Antiquity," http://bibleinteract.com/newsletter_teaching/the-stigma-of-infertility-in-antiquity/; accessed October 2017.

6. Public Domain.

7. Arthur Smith, "The Fourth Man," http://artists.letssingit.com/statler-brothers-lyrics-the-fourth-man-3z8kkmf#ixzz20uloRyUR, accessed July 2012.

8. Mark Batterson, *The Circle Maker* (Grand Rapids, MI: Zondervan), 84.

9. https://teenchallenge.cc/history-of-teen-challenge/; accessed October 2017.

10. "Abraham," Jewish Virtual Library, http://www.jewishvirtuallibrary.org/jsource/biography/abraham.html; accessed July 2012.

11. Aaron Marten, "Naomi, a Loving Mother-in-law," http://www.heraldmag.org/2003/03so_4.htm; accessed October 2017.

12. Norman Grubb, *Rees Howells Intercessor* (Fort Washington, PA: CLC Publications, 1952), 238–239.

13. Ibid, 239, 243.

14. Ibid, 283.

15. "Great Quotes on Prayer," https://thelife.com/great-quotes-on-prayer

16. <?> Charles John Ellicott, *Ellicott's Commentary on the Whole Bible*; http://www.biblesupport.com/e-sword-downloads/file/9937-ellicott-charles-j-commentary-on-the-whole-bible/; accessed September 2017.

17. Carter Conlon, Times Square Church, New York City, NY, January 2008, http://www.tscnyc.org/sermons/1172_764_0801_carter_conlon_the_deep_groanings_of_the_righteous.pdf; accessed October 2017.

18. Michael J. Svigel, "The Problem with Prayer," http://www.insight.org/resources/article-library/individual/the-problem-with-prayer; accessed September 2017.

19. Batterson, 127.

20. Dr. Ken Matto, "When You Are On The Backside Of The Desert," http://scionofzion.com/backside.htm; accessed October 2017.

21. In 1986, Bill became the second sitting member of the United States Congress to fly in space, as a payload specialist on the Space Shuttle *Columbia*. http://en.wikipedia.org/wiki/Bill_Nelson; accessed June 2017.

22. Jamie Buckingham, *A Way Through the Wilderness* (Palm Bay, FL: Risky Living Ministries, Inc., 1986), 42.

23. Ben Helmer, "The Prayer that Never Fails," http://stjohnscamden.org/the-prayer-that-never-fails/; accessed October 2017.

24. Charles R. Swindoll, "Strengthening Your Grip on Prayer," https://www.insight.org/resources/article-library/individual/strengthening-your-grip-on-prayer; accessed October 2017.

25. *Vine's* et al., Vol. 1, sv.v., "Together," 263.

26. Andrew Murray, "The Power of United Prayer," http://believersweb.org/view.cfm?ID=305; accessed September 2017. Living Ministries, Inc., 1986), 42.

27. Dr. Charles Swindoll, "Strengthening Your Grip on Prayer," https://www.insight.org/resources/article-library/individual/strengthening-your-grip-on-prayer; accessed October 2017.

28. Vine et al., Vol. 1, sv.v., "Together," 263.

29. Andrew Murray, "The Power of United Prayer," http://believersweb

30. John MacArthur, "The Righteous Anger of Jesus," https://www.gty.org/library/bibleqnas-library/QA0254/the-righteous-anger-of-jesus; accessed April 2016.

31. Charles Swindoll, "The Gathering Storm," http://www.insight.org/resources/article-library/individual/the-gathering-storm; accessed July 2015.

32. Eric Lenhart, "Jesus Clears the Temple," http://www.sermoncentral.com/sermons/monday-8211-8220jesus-clears-the-temple8221-eric-lenhart-sermon-on-passion-of-christ-149286.asp?Page=1; accessed April 2016.

33. Jerusalem Prayer Team Petition to President George W. Bush, JPT archives, used by permission.

34. Corrie ten Boom, with John and Elizabeth Sherrill, *The Hiding Place* (Old Tappan, NJ: Spire Books, 1971), 61.

35. Ibid, 67.

36. Ibid, 63.

37. Grubb, 283.

38. Sherrill, 101.

39. See Matthew 4.

40. William Shakespeare, *The Tragedy of Macbeth, Act 5, Scene 1,* http://shakespeare.mit.edu/macbeth/macbeth.5.1.html; accessed October 2017.

41. Batterson, 40.

42. William Shakespeare, *Hamlet Act 3, Scene 1*

43. "Secrets To God's Blessings," https://www.sermoncentral.com/sermons/secrets-to-gods-blessings-paul-fritz-sermon-on-gods-provision-78995?page=1; accessed September 2017.

44. Public Domain.

45. Max Lucado, "What Was Meant for Evil, God Uses for Good," September 30, 2013, http://www.faithgateway.com/what-was-meant-for-evil-god-uses-for-good/#.VH4jCo10w3E; accessed December 2014.

46. Francis McGaw, *John Hyde: The Apostle of Prayer* (Minneapolis, MN: Bethany House Publishers, 1970), 44.

47. Dr. Charles Stanley, http://www.christianitytoday.com/ct/2016/september-web-only/charles-stanley.html; accessed October 2017.

48. https://www.goodreads.com/quotes/tag/prayer; accessed October 2017.

49. Ibid.

50. McGaw, 48.

51. Public Domain.

BOOKS BY: MIKE EVANS

Israel: America's Key to Survival
Save Jerusalem
The Return
Jerusalem D.C.
Purity and Peace of Mind
Who Cries for the Hurting?
Living Fear Free
I Shall Not Want
Let My People Go
Jerusalem Betrayed
Seven Years of Shaking: A Vision
The Nuclear Bomb of Islam
Jerusalem Prophecies
Pray For Peace of Jerusalem
America's War:
 The Beginning of the End
The Jerusalem Scroll
The Prayer of David
The Unanswered Prayers of Jesus
God Wrestling
The American Prophecies
Beyond Iraq: The Next Move
The Final Move beyond Iraq
Showdown with Nuclear Iran
Jimmy Carter: The Liberal Left
 and World Chaos
Atomic Iran

Cursed
Betrayed
The Light
Corrie's Reflections & Meditations
The Revolution
The Final Generation
Seven Days
The Locket
Persia: The Final Jihad

GAMECHANGER SERIES:

GameChanger
Samson Option
The Four Horsemen

THE PROTOCOLS SERIES:

The Protocols
The Candidate

Jerusalem
The History of Christian Zionism
Countdown
Ten Boom: Betsie, Promise of God
Commanded Blessing
Born Again: 1948
Born Again: 1967
Presidents in Prophecy
Stand with Israel
Prayer, Power and Purpose

Turning Your Pain Into Gain

Christopher Columbus, Secret Jew

Living in the F.O.G.

Finding Favor with God

Finding Favor with Man

Unleashing God's Favor

The Jewish State: The Volunteers

See You in New York

Friends of Zion: Patterson & Wingate

The Columbus Code

The Temple

Satan, You Can't Have My Country!

Satan, You Can't Have Israel!

Lights in the Darkness

The Seven Feasts of Israel

Netanyahu

Jew-Hatred and the Church

The Visionaries

Why Was I Born?

Son, I Love You

Jerusalem DC (David's Capital)

Israel Reborn

Prayer: A Conversation with God

COMING SOON:

Shimon Peres: A Friend of Zion

The New Hitler

TO PURCHASE, CONTACT: orders@timeworthybooks.com
P. O. BOX 30000, PHOENIX, AZ 85046

MICHAEL DAVID EVANS, the #1 *New York Times* bestselling author, is an award-winning journalist/Middle East analyst. Dr. Evans has appeared on hundreds of network television and radio shows including *Good Morning America, Crossfire* and *Nightline*, and *The Rush Limbaugh Show*, and on Fox Network, *CNN World News*, NBC, ABC, and CBS. His articles have been published in the *Wall Street Journal, USA Today, Washington Times, Jerusalem Post* and newspapers worldwide. More than twenty-five million copies of his books are in print, and he is the award-winning producer of nine documentaries based on his books.

Dr. Evans is considered one of the world's leading experts on Israel and the Middle East, and is one of the most sought-after speakers on that subject. He is the chairman of the board of the ten Boom Holocaust Museum in Haarlem, Holland, and is the founder of Israel's first Christian museum located in the Friends of Zion Heritage Center in Jerusalem.

Dr. Evans has authored a number of books including: *History of Christian Zionism, Showdown with Nuclear Iran, Atomic Iran, The Next Move Beyond Iraq, The Final Move Beyond Iraq,* and *Countdown*. His body of work also includes the novels *Seven Days, GameChanger, The Samson Option, The Four Horsemen, The Locket, Born Again: 1967,* and *The Columbus Code*.

✦ ✦ ✦

Michael David Evans is available to speak or for interviews.
Contact: EVENTS@drmichaeldevans.com.